AF531472

INDIA BOOKVARSITY

LOTUS CHOICES

Editor: Mahendra Kulasrestha

The Golden Book of HINDUISM

A Multi-idea and Multi-layered Religio - Cultural Family

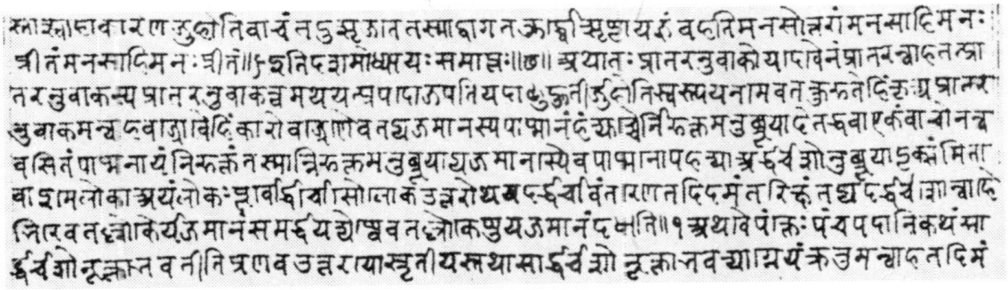

VEDIC PAPER MS. FROM THE BODLEIAN LIBRARY

In Devandgari Script

Classics Revived for an Ultramodern World

"In India, our religion will now and never strike root; the primitive wisdom of the human race will never be pushed aside there by the events of Galilee. On the contrary, Indian Wisdom will flow back upon Europe, and produce a thorough change in our knowing and thinking."

— Arthur Schopenhauer

An authentic survey of Hinduism till modern times and selections from major scriptures,

THE VEDAS, UPANISHADS and BHAGAVADGITA

4263/3, Ansari Road,
Darya Ganj, New Delhi- 110002

The Golden Book of HINDUISM

The Survey of Hinduism by J.N. FARQUHAR; and translations of scriptures by R.T.H. GRIFFITH, F. MAX MULLER and EDWIN ARNOLD

Sources:
A Primer of Hinduism,
by J.N. Farquhar,
Published by Oxford University Press, U.K. 1904

Sacred Books of the East
Edited by F. Max Muller,
Published by Clarendon Press,
Oxford, U.K., in the 1880s

The Song Celestial
by Edwin Arnold, 1885

and **Seven Great Religions**
by Annie Besant,
The Theosophical Publishing
House, Adyar, Chennai

The Golden Book of HINDUISM

First Edition—2009

ISBN: 81-8382-190-1 (H/B)

Published by:
Lotus Press
4263/3, Ansari Road, Darya Ganj,
New Delhi-10002
Ph.: 32903912, 23280047
E-mail: lotus_press@sify.com
www.lotuspress.co.in

Laser Typeset by: **Mala Sharma at Upasana Graphics**, Delhi

Printed at: **Saras Graphics**, Delhi

Editorspeak

A Class in Itself

Human life on the planet is distinct in the respect, that it has a fully developed brain in comparison to millions of other life-varieties. He exists because he thinks, and finds to his amazement, even horror, if one takes the liberty of going deeper and be more objective—that though his body-structure has immense potential, there are few opportunities to work it out; most of his time is wasted in acquiring food to fill his belly, large than any of the body part; that food is not available like air and water; that a greater part of humanity lives in hunger and poverty all its life. That there seems to be no clear meaning and/or purpose of life given to us without our asking or any kind of warning.

Gautam Buddha was quite correct in declaring life as essentially a 'suffering' so many years ago. He had hit the nail right on life's head, where it was needed, and for this reason, doubting God's existence; though he did not pursue this point to its logical ends as done by Jain thinkers, enumerating tens of reasons why God does not exist, in the 'Adi Purana'.

So, life being a very dark domain where its purpose was concerned, which was so conspicuously and blatantly missing, and there being lots of suffering, even undeserved, during its being lived, humanity needed a strong stick to hold tight in order to move along. This was, and is, Religion. People invented one God or more gods, which, perhaps, was, and is, their greatest invention. Both will remain so, until, well . . .

No other living being has any of these for the simple reason that they do feel but can't think and must suffer in silence.

Religions have been and are, many, and all of them have different characteristics. Every community gave shape to its religion in accord with its needs and circumstances. It is wrong to assume and declare that all religions are similar and teach the same things. No. Some religions believe in God and some do not; a few do not understand even the concept of God; some are very and some a little less violent, some are very very non violent, a few are in between. Some, like the great country China, did not develop any religion worth its name, and made extremely good with a neighbour's religion. Some religions are fanatically strict in their rules, some are not, others are in between.

So there are so many varieties, with their large set of rituals, friendly or enemical to this or that religion, and all very sacrosanct, permitting no criticism whatsoever by anyone. Comparative Religion is a very delicate academic subject, to be handled most cautiously, in all cases trying to save your neck as a basic must.

I'll therefore present here the case of one religion only, which is no more and there is no danger from that side. I myself didn't know much about it till a couple of months ago, when I visited my son in England and had the opportunity to read a few new books.

This is about the Aztec-Inca-Maya group of Mesoamerican religions. One would'nt believe that they sacrificed a large contingent of men every day so that the Sun would rise in the morning. Their religion told them that unless they will do so, the God will not come up and they will all die. On special occasions they sacrificed as many as 20,000 persons each day. The remarkable History Channel is doing excellent work in the area and presenting detailed records in their movies, about how they were laid on the stone and their heart taken out and offered to gods in all four directions, how other organs of the body were cut and used, how the skulls were kept — you can see these in modern museums kept in boxes in rows one after the other. Gory in the extreme, indeed!

This is an unbelievably ridiculous as well as violent example of Religion. Do we need one like it any more?

The story of the pagan Greek, as also its copycat Roman, religions is relatively well known, whose gods, including their chief, Zeus, were shameless 'fornicators', and the culture derived from them specialised in 'killing and drinking'. I've always wondered why they have been adorned as 'great', including Alexander, history's first villain.

Religion in modern times can be divided into a few groups: (1) the first group is a strict believer in God, and has one single root: Judaism, Christianity and Islam. They were born in the same land area, though they spread worldwide and had their direct impact on history; (2) the non-violent religions born in India, Jainism and Buddhism, the latter of which spread all over Asia, and still draws attention for its message of peace; and (3) the Hindu group of religions.

Added to these, the religion of Zarathustra, the Parsi religion, was an important religion of ancient times. Parts of it were Aryan, but it was destroyed almost in toto by Muslim attackers and had to take shelter in India.

Hinduism, the subject of the present work, is different from all these. For one, it is no single entity. In fact, the very word denotes a land, and that too, in an incorrect form—the original is 'Sindhu' which was spoken as 'Hindu' by barbarian invaders because their pronunciation faculties were not exact; and which has now been changed to 'Ind' – Indus, India – by the next group of invaders who came disguised as traders.

Two, the base of Hinduism is philosophical, to the extent of being overmuch argumentative–as the Nobel laureate Amartya Sen calls it. This gave rise to the concepts of Atman and Brahman, which Paul Deussen regards as our special contribution to world thought at such an early age. The Vedas start by looking at forces of nature, delving deeper into the idea of Purusha as the creator, which was soon developed by the Upanishads into a philosophy, perhaps the most systematic and comprehensive in all cultures. There are over 200 Upanishads primarily devoted to these discussions.

The Vedas were instrumental in developing the *yajnas* also in very elaborate form, as depicted in the Brahmana literature, but that turned out to be a passing phase, and were soon rejected as well as forgotten. There is no Brahmana in print in the market today and we don't know much about them. When bloody sacrifices, including human, were common practice in other parts of the world, we ran a parallel current of very non-violent religions, Jainism and Buddhism, which were absorbed by Hinduism as time passed.

The Upanishads were the high watermark of Hinduism, but these were not easily understandable to the masses, so a people's version was created in the Puranas. Avataras of God, their images, temples, elaborate cheerful ritual, and festivals and ceremonies grew into an overwhelming culture which continues unabated till date.

Hinduism has several prominent traditions of worship: the Siva tradition in its phallic as well as Mahadev image form; the Vishnu tradition, with Sri Rama and Sri Krishna as the most prominent deities; the Shakti or the goddess form, with Durga and Kali as most prominent, but many many more in various parts of the country, and the significant distinction that ours is the only land where the female is being worshipped; and the Tantric, Right as well as Left, based chiefly on the awakening of the huge energies of sex, again, a most unusual dimension of Hindu religion, which has been projected through the famous temples of Khajuraho, Konark, etc.

Hinduism is a multisided and multi-layered religio-cultural very large group, which, to my mind, also includes Buddhism and Jainism, and now Sikhism also — I like these too much and regard them as further expressions of our land's Truth, which cannot be overlooked and are equally relevant in modern turbulent times. If I am required to plan an eclectic religion to serve all humankind, I'll give their concepts of Non-violence and Compassion to all living beings the pride of place, for every intelligent person to follow.

Of late, Jesus Christ has come to be regarded as essentially Buddhist, who came to and studied in India when he was young, and returned to Kashmir after his crucifixion — in which event he is said to have been saved — where he lived till age 90, and where, on the outskirts of Srinagar, his resting place still exists — and which, the present writer has also been lucky to visit. There is now a good quantity of literature, descriptive as well as research-based, which cannot be ignored, though many may prefer to keep silent about it.

If that is so, and if Jesus can be set in the Bodhisattva tradition, like the traditions of China, Japan, etc., and if St. Paul, who took up the cause of Christianity and propagated it in Europe, could be firmly repudiated as non-Christ — because he was unaware of the truth and had only the Jewish ideas to propagate, he was not at fault in any perceivable manner — we would be tempted to include him and his religion also in this group.

Tolerance is a key ethical feature of Hinduism; Vivekananda has expanded it into 'acceptance' of every religion.

Hindu religions do not proselytise — the chief culprit of religious antagonism.

Theism in Hinduism is of various kinds; atheism is equally acceptable–in fact, it is the door to further research into the aspects of Truth.

Hinduism is a mixed and therefore almost complete religio-philosophical and socio-cultural all consuming phenomenon, with something for everybody in varying circumstances, catering to varying abilities and capabilities, aiming at a world family–*Vasudhaiva Kutumbakam*–which is now in the process of happening, and which has also the potential to change and grow with time. The outline of a world religion has already been drawn and presented by Vivekananda, which can now be seriously taken up.

This book has been culled from 'A Primer of Hinduism' by J.N. Farquhar, who was the literary secretary of Y.M.C.A in India and Ceylon in his time, and wrote it to facilitate conversion of Hindus to Christianity, so that the preachers could understand their targets better; he had predicted that later than sooner, this will suddenly but certainly happen. Though his forecast didn't come true, I find his writings most perceptive as well as honest – therefore I've preferred it over others. It were in fact the Christian missionaries who contributed an enormous lot to the resurgence of India and projected it to the world at large. Max Muller was one of them. My sincere thanks and regards to them.

I'll conclude this presentative note by quoting the famous historian A.L. Basham, who in his 'The Wonder That Was India' writes: 'Our overall impression is that in no other part of the ancient world were the relations of man and man, and of man and the state, so fair and humane. In no other early civilisation were slaves so few is number. Hindu India has few tales to tell of cities put to the sword or of the massacre of non-combatants. The ghastly sadism of the kings of Assyria, who flayed their captives alive, is completely without parallel in ancient India. To us the most striking feature of ancient Indian civilsation is its humanity.'

The introductory article to the 'Select Scriptures' has been culled from a lecture by the well known scholar and freedom-fighter, Annie Besant. It presents the rather complicated subject of Indian philosophy of Atman and Brahman in a most masterly manner, which took care of one of my singular worries about this book.

■ Editorspeak

Contents

Hindu ethos, Hail!

'... The genius of this country lies in its Hindu ethos ... The average Hindu you meet in a million villages possesses this simple innate spirituality and accepts your diversity, whether you are Christian or Muslim, Jain or Arab, French or Chinese ... They believed that the divine could manifest itself in different scriptures .... They had also given refuge to present minorities from across the world-syrian Christians, Parsis, Jews, Armenians, and today, Tibetans. In 3500 years of existence, Hindus have never militarily invaded another country and never tried to impose their religion on others by force or induced conversions ... (They) since the first Arab invasions have been at the receiving end of terrorism ... whom the Mahatma once gently called cowards ... They form one of the most successful, law-abiding and integrated communities in the world today.'

—Francois Gautier

Editor-in-Chief,

La Revue de l'Inde, Paris

(**Outlook**, 30 Nov. 08)

The River of Hinduism

The Image of a Hindu

•

Hinduism through the Ages

•

Hinduism Now

The Image of a Hindu

A MAN is a Hindu because of two things, birth and conformity. In order to be a Hindu, a man must have been born in one of the social groups which historically have become associated together in Hinduism, and which are known as castes. A man born in Hinduism must conform to the usages of the group in which he was born. The customs of the various castes vary to an extraordinary degree. In some castes a great many things are obligatory, in others comparatively few.

The rules about marriage are the most fundamental part of caste. To marry outside one's caste is forbidden, usually choice is further narrowed to one section or sub-caste; and even within this subdivision there are the further restrictions of *pravara* and *gotra*. Rules with regard to food restrict the articles of diet that may be eaten, the persons by whom food may be cooked, and the persons with whom it may be eaten. Educated men in the large cities usually keep caste rules in their own homes, but disregard them outside. Rules about occupation are in general very loose and easy among the educated classes, but stringent where modern thought has not penetrated. An educated man may usually take up any occupation he pleases.

The observance of certain domestic ceremonies is binding on every man who wishes to remain a Hindu. They are carried out with care in every family under the guidance of Brahmin priests. In the code of Manu, as in the older sacred books, twelve domestic rites or sacraments, *sanskaras*, are prescribed for the twice-born castes:

(1) *Garbhadhana,* impregnation, following the marriage ceremony.

(2) *Pumsavana,* male-production, about three months after marriage.

(3) *Simantonnayana,* hair-parting, the parting of the woman's hair some time before the birth of her child.

(4) *Jatakarma,* birth-ceremony.

(5) *Namakarana,* namegiving.

(6) *Nishkramana,* carrymg-out. In the fourth month the child is carried out to look on the rising sun.

(7) *Annaprasana,* food-giving.

(8) *Chauda,* tonsure.

(9) *Kesanta,* hair-cutting.

(10) *Upanayana,* initiation, the ceremony which introduces the boy to his education.

(11) *Samavartana,* home-coming, the return of the student to his home from the house of his teacher.

(12) *Vivaha,* marriage.

To-day the twice-born castes usually observe only the following :

(5) *Nama-karana,* narne-giving.

(7) *Anna-prasana,* food-giving.

(10) *Upanayana,* initiation.

(12) *Vivaha,* marriage.

The other castes have corresponding ceremonies.

The Hindu family is patriarchal in form. Modern customs differ a good deal in detail from the customs of the Rigvedic and earlier ages, yet in the main the ideas and the practice are the same.

The ceremonies connected with the burning of the dead do not, in the opinion of modern Hindus, come under the head of ancestor-worship. All primitive peoples believe that whoever touches a dead body is defiled thereby, and this idea still survives in Hinduism. Hence the burning of the dead which is called *antyeshti*, the last stacrifice, is polluting, the worship of ancestors is called *sraddha*, an act of faith, and all the ceremonies that come under that head are auspicious.

The Funeral Ceremonies last ten days. The essential element in each day's ceremony is the offering of a *pinda*, i.e., a ball of cooked rice, to the spirit of the deceased. The belief is that the spirit of the deceased through feeding on this food acquires a gross body, *sthula sarira*, and is thereby transformed from a *preta* or wandering ghost into a *pitri*, father.

Sraddha Ceremonies—A man's relatives, male and female, on both his father's and his mother's side, for three generations upward and three generations downward, are called his *sapindas*, i.e., sharers in the *pinda*, because they take part in the *sraddha* ceremonies with him. On the eleventh day, all the *sapindas* gather in the house of the person who is holding the ceremony, and an elaborate ceremony is conducted the central element of which is the offering of a *pinda* to every deceased person within the circle of *sapindas*. A feast follows the ceremony.

This is repeated monthly for one year, and then annually.

Rules about worship vary very much amongst the lower castes of Hinduism, but among the upper castes they run on the following lines:

Daily prayers, connected with bathing and teeth-cleaning, and daily sacrifices. These are all observed by strictly orthodox Hindus, but are often neglected by educated men.

The daily worship of the household gods. Usually the women see to this.

The recurrent festivals, fasts and holy days. These vary very greatly in different parts of the country and in the different sects. No Hindu can avoid taking part in these from time to time.

The worship at the temple. This takes a large place in the lives of all Hindus except modern educated men, who seldom go near a temple at all, at least in the North.

Belief is altogether free. A Hindu is generally understood to believe that the Vedas are inspired, that the Brahmins are divinely appointed priests, and that caste is a divine institution, but **a man may declare that he believes none of these things and yet remain a good Hindu, provided he conforms.** Yet the stability of Hinduism depends in the last resort on the existence of these beliefs. The Vedas are quoted frequently in the domestic ceremonies, and the presence of Brahmins is necessarry for the right performance of each one of them.

Although Hinduism has many gods, many theologies, and many sacred books, a man remains a Hindu without believing in any god or any theology, and without knowing or acknowledging a single sacred book. He must give some sort of practical recognition to some god or gods in the domestic ceremonies and family festivals but the divinities thus reverenced vary all over India; there is no uniformity. Nor are there any theological conceptions which he need hold: an orthodox Hindu may be an atheist, or an agnostic. The sacred books of Hinduism are not read in the services of the temples, nor is the ordinary Hindu expected to study them. The Ramayana and the Mahabharata, however, are very largely read in the homes of the people.

But although there is no set of beliefs which the Hindu as a Hindu is expected to hold, there are certain ideas or convictions which all or nearly all Hindus will be found to hold. They are, first, the validity of caste and the authority of the Vedas and the Brahmins; second, the doctrine of transmigration; and third, the sacredness of the cow.

Perhaps it may be said that a further general characteristic of Hinduism is to be found in a tendency of thought, feeling, and aspiration of which the logical issue is a mystic pantheism.

Most Hindus are also touched at least in some degree with ascetic ideas. The villager, no matter how worldly his own life may be, is ready to affirm that the things of the world are worthless, nothing is of any final value except God and the knowledge of God. He therefore holds that the man who does not give up the world in its entirety and become an ascetic does not really love God. He regards the preservation of animal life (*ahimsa*) as meritorious.

Though the simplest Hindu is ready to express belief in one God only, his practical daily religion is a very vivid conviction that the idol in his village is alive, and not only eats, drinks, and sleeps but has power to bless or curse him in every detail of his life. Vishnu is believed to be present in great power in every *salagrama* stone, a kind of black ammonite found in rivers, and in every *tulsi* plant. Siva and the other gods have similar superstitions attached to them. Indeed there is no limit to the animals, trees, stones rivers, and wells in which divinities are believed to reside. The belief in holy places is vigorous.

The lower orders of the population of India fall into two classes, those who have lived in close contact with Hindu society, and those who have lived apart in the mountains and forests. The latter have retained their old religion and social organization, but the former have all succumbed to the influence of caste and have absorbed large elements of Hindu theology, mythology, and superstition.

There are vast multitudes of people both north and south who are regarded as unclean, who in consequence are excluded from all Brahminical temples, and for whom no Brahmin will perform any ceremony. But they have come so largely under Hindu influence that they cannot be truly excluded. They show this Hindu influence first of all in their caste organization and in their social usages, which are very largely an imitation of high-caste practice; secondly, in their belief in Hindu theology and superstition, and their desire to bring their village divinites into some sort of relation to the gods of the Hindu pantheon.

The lowest of these castes are held in such abhorrence that they are not allowed to live beside the higher castes. They form villages for themselves. Both of these Hinduised groups are inclined to pay worship to the lower divinities of Hinduism and Kali, the black, bloodthirsty, goddess of the North, other divine animals, and the divine serpents called Nagas.

But the worship to which the ignorant Indian villager clings with most fervour is just the village divinity. These are found all over India, varying everywhere, yet retaining certain broad similarities everywhere. The priests of these divinities are not Brahmins, but men of all castes.

The great majority of these divinities are goddesses. In the South almost everyone has the word *amma,* 'mother,' in her name. They are propitiated rather than adored. Visitations of disease, famine, earthquake, are attributed to them; and special sacrifices and festivals are held to induce them to remove the scourge. Animals are usually sacrificed to them on these occasions, fowls, sheep, goats, pigs, and buffaloes.

The shrines of these divinities are of the rudest description, often only a small piece of land marked off by lines of stones. Frequently, there is no symbol of the god at all; often a stained stone is set up; often a rude image. The people suffer greatly from their fear of evil spirits; insomuch that a very large part of their religion consists in efforts to drive them away or to nullify their influence.

Hinduism through the Ages

The Aryan People

In the dim background of history we catch misty glimpses of a great people which had a common culture, a common religion, and a common language, but, which in the following centuries through division and migration split up into many groups and thus **produced a large number of the leading nations of Europe and of Asia.** In the language, religion, and life of their descendants we can still find traces of the common life lived so long ago by the Aryan race.

Careful comparison of the religions of the various ancient Aryan peoples enables us to realize in some degree what the religion was in the still earlier days of the undivided people. It seems certain, first of all, that **they honoured a vast number of special gods, each of them supposed to oversee some distinct aspect of life.** But in that primitive age these Aryan men had already another group of gods distinguished as the heavenly ones *(deva—deus)* from the vulgar throng. They were all natural phenomena, but they were also all connected one way or another with the sky and with the grandest of nature's operations. It seems clear that the undivided people already worshipped Sky, Sun, Moon, Dawn, Wind, Fire. But though they regarded and worshipped them as gods, they still called them by their significant names; they had not given them proper names or epithets, The usual method of obtaining the help of the gods in those days seems to have been already prayer and sacrifice of a rudimentary kind. In both prayer and sacrifice true religious feeling mingled with belief in the occult power of charmed words and deeds. It was believed that special knowledge was required for both prayer and sacrifice. Hence, the man of skill in these important matters was a person of consequence. The Latin word *flamen* and the Sanskrit *brahman* seem both to go back to the Aryan original which was used to designate this embryo priest. The earliest form of sacrifice consisted merely in laying out food and drink on the ground for the gods to come and enjoy.

Ancestor-worship was almost as important to the original Aryan people as the worship of the gods. Uncivilised people usually believe that the soul survives death and lives a new life apart from the body. But early man, not having been able to reach the idea of spirit as distinct from material substance, conceives the soul as a material thing, and believes that after death it is dependent for its continued existence on food and drink precisely like a living man. In consequence of this, nearly all primitive races have been accustomed to provide food and drink for the departed souls of members of their own family. The food is laid out as for a feast, and the souls of the dead are invited to come and eat and be nourished thereby. We must note that this practice, which is all but universal among the simpler peoples, is a service of souls and not a worship. The dead are dependent on the family for their nourishment.

But these beliefs have passed among many peoples into a more developed stage, where the dead are conceived as being powerful beings, controlling the welfare of the family. When this idea arises, the old service of the dead becomes a worship. The family pays them great reverence, not merely because they are relatives, but in order to secure their loving care over the family. This form of worship, then, had been developed before the original Aryan race split up.

The father was the high-priest of the family, and controlled the worship of the ancestors of the family in all details. He alone knew the peculiar ritual which was traditional in his family, and which had to be maintained unchanged, if favour of the dead was to be retained. He alone had the power to pass on the rites to his son. As high-priest of the ancestral rites he was the acknowledged head of the family. The reverence and the power which his priestly position brought him, made him supreme in the home. He had full power over his wife and his young children, and in many of the nations of a later date his grown-up sons also were completely under his authority. The property of the family was altogether in his hands. This is the source of the *patria potestas* of Rome, and of the prominent place held by the father in Greece, Persia, India, and among Teutonic and Slavonic peoples as well.

This type of family, which is known as the patriarchal, succeeded an earlier and less developed type; and the changed form of family life produced great and far-reaching results. The first of these was a new consciousness of the unity, sanctity, and value of the family; and this new and lofty conception produced in turn a great advance in family morality, in family feeling, and family pride. Marriage became universal; for every man wanted a son to take over the worship of the ancestors at his death. Since the father was supreme, and since every family wanted sons, there was a tendency to set less value on woman. In consequence many girl babies were exposed or put to death in every race practising ancestor-worship; and a woman was held to be of far less account than a man.

The Indo-Iranian People

A certain portion of the mighty Aryan family broke away from the main stock—we do not know when or where—and remained a united people for some time, but finally fell in two; one taking up its abode in Iran, the other moving into the territory on both sides of the upper Indus. These people, the ancestors of the Zoroastrians and of the creators of Hinduism, may be designated Indo-Iraian during the period while they were still one. By inference from the Vedas, the earliest literature of India, on the one hand, and from the *Avesta* and other Iranian records on the other, we are able to realize in hazy outline what the religion of this prehistoric people was. The *Avesta* is the literature produced by Zoroaster and his friends in the great reformation carried out by them ahout 600 B.C., but it contains many older elements.

Clearly considerable advance had been made in conceiving the heavenly gods; for there is now quite a group of personalised divinities with definite names and lofty functions. It seems clear that the following at least were fully recognised, Varuna, Mitra, Aryaman, Bhaga, and Indra, and along with them Yama and Soma. Theology had made a good deal of progress; for they are thought of as spiritual beings, and the natural phenomena from which they originally sprang are now but the medium of their manifestation.

The sacrifice, meanwhile, had been greatly elaborated. A ritual had been established, and hymns as well as prayers accompanied the stated acts. The home of the gods being now consistently believed to be in heaven, it was the common practice to send the sacrifice to them on the flames and smoke of the altar fire. The drink of the gods offered in sacrifice is the juice of a plant called *soma* in Sanskrit, *haoma* in Zend, the language of the *Avesta.* A special ritual for the offering of this divine drink had appeared, and the drink itself had undergone apotheosis. *Soma* is already a god. The priests, too, have now far fuller functions and are called by special names.

The belief about the dead had also made considerable progress. **Burning had almost universally taken the**

place of burying probably from a wish to release the soul as completely as possible from the body and to bear it away on the flame of the pyre to the heavenly regions. For when men die, they are believed to go to heaven, where they join the blessed dead and enjoy immortality with the gods. They are invited to the sacrifices in the same way as the gods. They are believed to be very powerful.

The Aryan Family of Languages

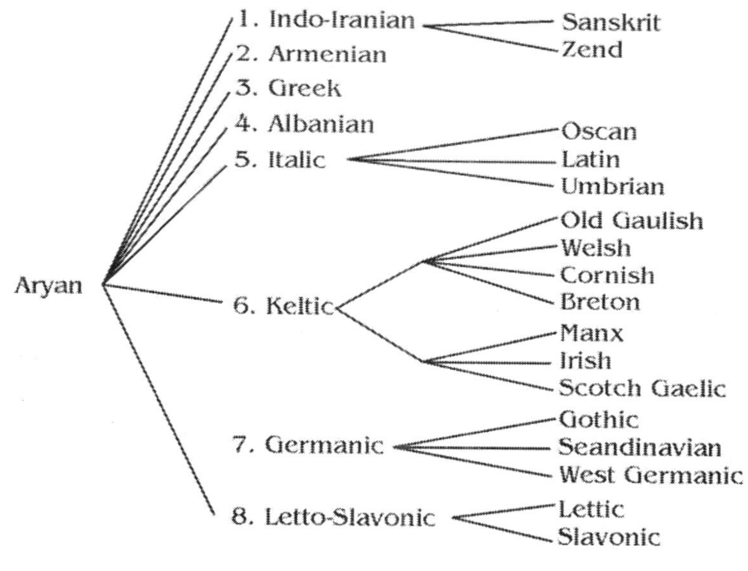

THE VEDAS

तत्सवितुर्वरेण्यं भर्गो देवस्य धीमहि धियो यो नः प्रचोदयात् ।।

That excellent glory of the Quickening Sun, the god, may we attain; may he stimulate our devotions.'

—Rigveda

History: Our first historical knowledge of the Aryan tribes which produced the great civilisation of India shows them settled in the Western Punjab and beyond the Indus. They were a tall, fair people. They gradually spread further east, as far as the district of Karnal, later known as the holy land of the Kurus, Kurukshetra. They were then soldier-farmers, equally used to the plough and the sword. They were constantly at war with the aborigines around them; and they looked eagerly for sunshine and rain to mature their crops and give them fodder for their cattle and herds. They were still a primitive people, living in simple villages, with but few of the arts of civilisation, and untrammelled by the bonds of caste. They had no writing and no coinage. The tribes lived each under its own chieftain, and now and then quarrels led to war among them. The family was still in a healthy condition. **Their women had a great deal of freedom throughout their lives. There was no child-marriage among them and no law against the remarriage of widows.** Like most peoples, they practised the exposure of children and old people.

Religion: Like their early Aryan ancestors, they worshipped the heavenly powers, calling them *devas;* and they were very conscious of the great advantage which their knowledge of these gods gave them over the aborigines. They arranged their gods in three groups, according as they belonged to the upper region of light, the atmosphere, or the earth. These three groups were designated Upper, Middle, and Lower. The chief divinities were—Upper: Varuna, Surya, Savitri, Vishnu, Ushas, Aditi, Mitra, Aryaman, the Asvins; Middle: Vata, Indra, Rudra, Parjanya, the Maruts; Lower: Agni, Soma, Yama.

Their worship was largely sacrificial. Animals were often killed in sacrifice; but their most elaborate rites were connected with the offering of the *Soma,* of which we have already heard, and of clarified butter, called *ghee.* They were accustomed to have hymns recited at all sacrifices. But, although they laid so much stress on sacrifice, **they had no temples and no images**. Sacrifices were offered in the open air, and the arrangements were very simple. The gods were so closely connected with natural phenomena that no visible symbol was required.

Already the people seem to have been roughly divided into three groups—warriors, priests, and agriculturists; but they were classes rather than castes. The priest, Brahmin, was already very influential; for he was believed to have great power over the gods. Every chieftain had his own Brahmin chaplain, *purohita,* whose help he sought before entering on any undertaking, The priests tended to become a caste; for they already made great pretensions and claimed exclusive powers. They were sub-divided into three orders, each of which had its own special duties to perform at the sacrifices. Already schools were in existence for the education of priests. In this fact lies one of the chief reasons for the extraordinary predominance which the Brahmins finally attained.

Austerity, called *tapas* in Sanskrit, was practised in those days. Various forms of self-torture were endured, with a view to securing warlike prowess, invincibility, miraculous powers, or heaven. The *muni,* who practised *tapas,* wore yellow robes.

The worship of ancestors was kept up with great care by the Indo-Aryans. They were called *pitaras,* 'fathers', were regularly worshipped, and were invited to come to the sacrifice along with the gods. After death it was believed that the souls ot the good were conducted by Yama to the place prepared for them, where they enjoyed an immortality of peace and happiness along with the 'fathers' and the gods. There was no doctrine of transmigration in those days.

Literature: By the end of this period the centre of Hindu culture had moved east with the moving tribes to the holy field of Kurukshetra. The hymns, which had been composed during the previous centuries, and which were carefully preserved in the great families and believed to be inspired, were now gradually gathered in some priestly schools into the great collection which is called the *Rigveda.* Young Brahmins committed these hymns to memory at school, in order to be able to use them at the sacrifices. The collection was universally accepted by the people as their sacred book, every hymn being recognised as a divine utterance revealed to the *rishi,* 'seer', whose name it bears.

Just before the collection was closed, a hymn was added which declares that the three great divisions of the people and the aboriginal Sudras had each a distinct origin in God. Thus a religious basis was found for that old-world form of fixed social organization which soon developed into caste.

These hymns which form the *Rigveda* are one of the most interesting groups of literature in all the world. **No other people ever produced a body of religious poetry of such striking originality and beauty at such an early stage of the history.** The nearest parallel is formed by the Zoroastrian *Gathas* or hymns of the *Avesta,* the earliest literature of the sister people, the Iranians or early Persians; but they have not nearly the interest and power of the *Rigveda,* The people in their daily life, their war, toil and worship, stand out clear and distinct in these hymns; and there is something most fascinating in the way the gods are received and addressed.

A few of the later hymns are philosophical. They ask questions rather than answer them; yet already the conception of the One behind all the gods finds expression, and a number of the ideas which afterwards helped to create the Hindu systems are tentatively put forward.

At a later date a large number of verses were gathered together, nearly all of them from the *Rigveda,* and so arranged as to form a special manual for the second order of priests. This collection was called the *Samaveda.* Its verses were chanted at the Soma sacrifice. Another manual, consisting partly of verses, partly of sacrificial formulae in prose, was put together for the use of the third order, and was called the *Yajurveda.* At a later date a new school separated the sacrificial formulae from the verses. The old *Yajurveda* was thereafter called Black, while the unmixed text was known as the White. These new collections were held to be divinely inspired just like the *Rigveda.* They were revelation in the fullest sense. The word for revelation is *sruti,* 'hearing.' When the second and third orders had each formed its own *Veda,* the *Rigveda* tended to become the manual of the first order only.

ब्राह्मणोऽस्य मुखमासीद्‌बाहू राजन्यः कृतः।
ऊरू तदस्य यद्वैश्यः पद्‌भ्यां शूद्रो अजायत।।

'The Brahmin was his (Purusha's) mouth; the Rajanya was made from his arms; his thighs became the Vaisya; from his feet the Sudra was produced.'

—Rigveda, X. xc. 12.

A Hymn to Agni, the Priest

Fire is one of the early Aryan gods. When it became customary to send the sacrifice to the gods by fire, Agni, the fire-god, became recognised by the Indo-Aryans as the Messenger of the sacrifice, the great Priest.

O worthy of oblation, Lord of prospering powers, assume thy robes, and offer this our sacrifice.

Sit, ever to be chosen, as our Priest, most youthful, through our hymns, O Agni, through our heavenly word.

For here a Father for his son, Kinsman for kinsman worshippeth, and Friend, choice-worthy, for his friend.

Here let the foe-destroyers sit, Varuna, Mitra, Aryaman, like men, upon our sacred grass.

O ancient Herald, be thou glad in this our rite and fellowship; hearken thou well to these our songs.

Whate'er in this perpetual course we sacrifice to god and god, that gift is offered up in thee.

May he be our dear household Lord, Priest, pleasant and choice-worthy; may we, with bright fires, be dear to him.

The gods, adored with brilliant fires, have granted precious wealth to us; so, with bright fires, we pray to thee.

And, O Immortal One, so may the eulogies of mortal men belong to us and thee alike.

With all thy fires, O Agni, find pleasure in this our sacrifice, and this our speech, O Son of Strength.

—*Rigveda,* I. xxvi

Funeral Hymn

The verses of this hymn are used in the Hindu funeral ceremony as it is prescribed in the Sutras.

Him who departed over the mighty mountains, and thus showed the path to many, the son of Vivasvant, the gatherer of the peoples, Yama the king; do thou honour with an oblation.

Yama first found a refuge for us; nor can that rich land be taken away. Whither our fathers of old time have gone, thither along their own paths the children go.

Go forth, go forth by the ancient paths whither our fathers of old time have gone. Thou shalt see both kings rejoicing in their bliss, Yama and Varuna the god.

Go join the Fathers, join Yama, and thy merit in highest heaven. Leaving thy imperfections, return to thy home, and, filled with life, join thy body.

Depart, separate and disperse, for him the Fathers have prepared this place; Yama grants him a place of rest, adorned with days and waters and nights.

By the straight path hasten thou past the two Sarameyan dogs, four-eyed, brindled. Then draw near the mindful Fathers, who revel in bliss with Yama.

And these two dogs of thine, Yama, warders, four-eyed, path-guardians, men-beholders, to them do thou entrust this man, O king, and bestow both health and wealth upon him.

—*Rigveda, X. xiv*

The Divisions of the Vedic People

1. *Brahmins:* prayermen, priests.

2. *Kshatriyas:* authoritymen, rulers and soldiers (called also *Rajanyas).*

3. *Vaisyas:* men of the people, agriculturists.

4. *Sudras:* aboriginal people brought under Brahmin authority.

The Three Orders of Brahmins

1. hotri= 'sacrificer'		from *hu*	= pour on the fire.
2. *udgatri*	= 'singer'	from *udgai*	= sing.
3. *adhvaryu*	= 'working priest'	from *adhvara*	= a ritual act.

The Vedas and their Names

the *hotri*	recites	*richas,*	'praises':	hence *Rigveda.*
the *udgatri*	raises	*samani,*	'chants':	hence *Samaveda.*
the *adhvaryu*	mutters	*yajumshi,*	'sacrificial formulae';	hence *Yajurveda.*

NOTE.—The word Veda means knowledge.

Growth of the Three Vedas

External Events	*History*	*Literature*		
	The Indo-Aryans on both sides of the Indus.	Gradual		
Israel leaves Egypt, about 1320 B.C.		Composition		
	The Priests divided into three Orders.	of		
Fall of Troy.		the		
	Rise of Priestly Education.	Hymns.		
David, King of Israel, about 1000 B.C.	The Indo-Aryans as far east as Kurukshetra.	Gradual Compliation of the *Rigveda*	Compliation of the *Samaveda*	Compliation of the *Yajurveda*
	Theory of the Four Castes.			

THE BRAHMANAS

द्वया वै देवावा।ः देवा अहैव देवाः। अथ ये
ब्राह्मणाः श्रुश्रुवांसोनूचानास्ते मनुष्यदेवाः।।

Verily, there are two kinds of gods; for, indeed, the gods are the gods; and the Brahmins who have studied and teach sacred lore are the human gods.'

—*Satapatha Brahmana, II. ii.*

The great question which we have to learn to answer at this point is: How did the simple people we have just heard of become the Hindus whom we know? The transformation took place as a result of two forces:

A Vanaprastha and his Hut, from the Bharhut Stupa.

(a) The gradual development of the culture of the people.

(b) The gradual conquest of India by them.

The conquest was carried out partly by war, but largely by the priests, who won over the tribes by their superior knowledge and culture. This chapter and the following will show how the simple faith of the *Rigveda* was transformed into the Hindu system.

History. The Aryans continued to advance eastwards during this period, leavening the old population as they went, until by its dose nearly the whole of North India had come under their government and civilisation. As they went, the Brahmins brought the aboriginal tribes under their priestly rule, giving each tribe a definite place in their social system, which was now steadily stiffening into caste. Thus many new caste-groups arose. The land was divided into a great many small kingdoms, most of them ruled by kings of Aryan race. Large trade sprang up; even sea voyages on the Indian Ocean were undertaken; and wealth increased. Through the intercourse of Indian sailors with merchants in Babylonia the art of writing was introduced; but for lack of suitable writing materials it was not used for literary purposes for many centuries. By the end of the period the patriarchal family had become more developed, and women were beginning to be looked down upon.

Religion. The extension and elaboration of the sacrificial system is what gives this period its religious character. While, in the times of the *Rigveda,* men sought to win the regard of the gods, or to persuade them to give their help by sacrifice, hymn and prayer, in this new period the sacrifice is regarded as a mysterious operation which, if faithfully carried out, will irresistibly compel the gods to grant the appropriate reward. If only carried far enough, sacrifices will exalt a man to the level of the gods. The accurate performance of every detail of the ritual thus became a matter of extreme importance.

For this reason the priest was all-powerful. His help was needed at every point in the intricate ceremonial of the altar. Without him the layman was helpless. Hence the divine authority of the Brahmin was fully acknowledged and became firmly rooted in the religious practice of the nation. Indeed, so great had the power of the priests become that they were spoken of as gods upon earth, and were feared even more than the gods of heaven. Fees paid to them were declared to be quite as meritorious as sacrifices offered to the celestials. All the old sacrifices were greatly extended and elaborated, so that no layman could conduct them with accuracy. It was during this period that the *Rajasuya,* or Coronation Sacrifice, the *Asvamedha,* or Horse Sacrifice, an assertion of imperial authority, the *Purushamedha,* or Human Sacrifice (but a substitute was used), and the other great sacrifices, took form and became famous.

Towards one God

During this period the theological ideas of the Brahmins underwent a great change. A deep tendency is manifested towards belief in one God, either the personal Creator, Prajapati or, more often, a mysterious incomprehensible divine essence diffused through all things. Along with this new God came the idea that the ordinary gods were merely mortals until they extorted immortality from the Supreme by sacrifice and austerity. Many of the ancient gods had already fallen into the background, while others had come into great prominence, among whom were Rudra, who now received his more attractive name, Siva, and Vishnu; Siva as the mountain-god and Vishnu as the sun-god.

Towards the end of this period we begin to meet a real order of ascetics. They lived in the forest and usually built themselves huts of wood or leaves. They were called *Vanaprasthas,* forest-dwellers, hermits, and a collection of their huts was called an *asrama,* hermitage. They wore coats of bark or skin, wound up their hair in matted coils, and lived largely on woodland fare.

A Meditation for the Vanaprastha

The Horse of the Asvamedha

Verily the dawn is the head of the horse which is fit for sacrifice, the sun its eye, the wind its breath, the mouth the Vaisvanara fire, the year the body of the sacrificial horse. Heaven is the back, the sky the belly, the earth the chest, the quarters the two sides, the intermediate quarters the ribs, the members the seasons, the joints the months and half months, the feet days and nights, the bones the stars, the flesh the clouds. The half-digested food is the sand, the rivers the bowels, the liver and the lungs the mountains, the hairs the herbs and trees. As the sun rises, it is the forepart, as it sets, the hindpart of the horse. When the horse shakes itself, then it lightens; when it kicks, it thunders; when it makes water, it rains; voice is its voice.

Verily Day arose after the horse as the golden vessel, called Mahiman, which at the sacrifice is placed before the horse. Its place is in the Eastern sea. The Night arose after the horse as the silver vessel, called Mahiman, which at the sacrifice is placed behind the horse. Its place is in the Western sea. Verily these two vessels arose to be on each side of the horse.

As a racer he carried the Devas, as a stallion the Gandharvas, as a runner the Asuras, as a horse men. The sea is its kin, the sea is its birthplace.

—*Brihadaranyaka Upanishad,* i. I:

The law of *ahimsa* (harmlessness), that they must not kill an animal nor break a living twig from a tree, gradually arose among them. They continued the worship of the gods and the worship of their ancestors, and they retained their place in the family and in caste, but did no work of any kind. They practised various methods of severe austerity, enduring extreme cold and heat, strange food, painful postures, and such like. The purpose of the endurance of this *tapas* was still in the main the attainment of miraculous powers; but moral aims now began to mingle with the older motives.

The Vanaprastha and the Asrama

When Rama, valiant hero, stood
In the vast shade of Dandak wood,
His eyes on every side he bent
And saw a hermit settlement,
Where coats of bark were hung around,
And holy grass bestrewed the ground.
Bright with Brahmanic lustre glowed
That circle where the saints abode:
Like the hot sun in heaven it shone,
Too dazzling to be looked upon.
Wild creatures found a refuge where
The court, well-swept, was bright and fair,
And countless birds and roedeer made
Their dwelling in the friendly shade.
Beneath the boughs of well-loved trees
Oft danced the gay Apsarases.
Around was many an ample shed
Wherein the holy fire was fed;
With sacred grass and skins of deer,
Ladles and sacrificial gear,

And roots and fruit, and wood to burn,
And many a brimming water-urn.
There, clad in coats of bark and hide—
Their food by roots and fruit supplied—
Dwelt many an old and reverend sire
Bright as the sun or Lord of Fire,
All with each worldly sense subdued,
A pure and saintly multitude.

—Valmiki, *Ramayana,* Book III, Canto i

Hermits seek purity of soul and nearness to God as well as power over gods and men. A special form of teaching called *aranyaka,* i.e., belonging to the forest, seems to have been given to young men who were about to enter upon the hermit life. The essential element in this forest-teaching was an attempt to spiritualise the sacrifice by means of allegory. This instruction would then form the basis of the hermit's meditation in the forest.

The Origin and the Power of Sacrifice

Now Prajapati the lord of creatures, having created living beings, felt himself as it were exhausted. The creatures turned away from him; the creatures did not abide with him for his joy and food.

He thought within him, 'I have exhausted myself, and the object for which I have created has not been accom-plished; my creatures have turned away from me, the creatures have not abode with me for my joy and food.'

Prajapati thought within him,' How can I again strengthen myself; the creatures might then return to me; the creatures might abide with me for my joy and food.'

He went on praising and toiling, desirous of creatures. He beheld that set of eleven victims. By offering therewith Prajapati again strengthened himself; the creatures returned

Two Vanaprasthas with their huts and the implements of fire-sacrifice in a hunting scene from the Buddhist Stupa at Sanchi

to him, his creatures abode for his joy and food. By offering he truly became better.

Therefore, then, let the sacrificer offer with the set of eleven victims, for thus he truly strengthens himself by offspring and cattle; the creatures turn unto him, the creatures abide with him for his joy and food; he truly becomes better by offering; therefore, then, let him offer with the set of eleven victims.

—*Satapatha Brahmana, III. ix.*

The aboriginal tribes were allowed to retain their gods and their old worship. A practical acknowledgement of the supremacy of the Brahmins and of Brahminic ideas was all that was demanded of them. Naturally, it the intercourse which thus sprang up, the aborigines learned much from the Aryans. On the other hand, a great many aboriginal ideas and many alien religious practices and conceptions found their way into the Vedic faith. The most important change thus produced was the movement of thought towards Transmigration. Snakes, trees, and pools were by this time held in great reverence, and pilgrimage was recognised as a meritorious religious practice.

Literature, etc. The priestly schools had now become great and learned associations, each with a tradition of its own; and so honoured were they that a man was proud to avow himself a member of his school. Every Brahmin had to pass through one of them, in order to qualify as a priest. He had to learn by heart the Veda which belonged to his order, and to receive from the lips of his teacher a great deal of detailed information, especially with regard to his work at the altar, the correct pronunciation of the sacred hymns and the meaning of certain acts and stories. Language-study had made considerable progress among them.

As time went on, the teaching given in each school took definite form and was handed down with great verbal accuracy from teacher to pupil. The oral tradition of a school was called the *Brahmana* of that school. From this point onward then each priest studied the *Veda* of his order and the *Brahmana* pertaining to it. Then as education advanced, a number of schools arose under each *Veda*, and differences, great and small, crept into the teaching, until each great school had its own *Brahmana*, usually called by the traditional name of the school. Thus arose the Brahmanas, the most uninteresting prose literature in all the world. They are, however; of considerable value historically; for they enable scholars to form a picture of the life and religion of the times.

The Chief Charanas or Schools with their Brahmanas

Charanas	*Brahmanas*
A. Rigveda—	
1. The Aitareyins · · ·	*Aitareya*
2. The Kaushitakins · ·	*Kaushitaki*
B. Samaveda—	
1. The Tandins · · · ·	*Panchavimsa*
2. The Chhandogyas · ·	*Chhandogya*
3. The Talavakaras · · ·	*Talavakara*
C. Black Yajur—	
1. The Taittiriyins · · ·	*Taittiriya*
2. The Kathakas	
3. The Maitrayaniyas	
White Yajur—	
1. The Vajasaneyins · ·	Satapatha
D. Atharvaveda—	
	Gopatha

The *Chhandogya Brahmana* has not survived, though we have the *Chhandogya Upanishad.*

Relative Age of the Brahmanas: Dates Unknown

External Events	*Indian History*	*Literature*	
Elijah, the Prophet, about 860 B.C.	The Aryans in Kurukshetra	THE BRAHMANAS	
The *Iliad* composed.	Elaboration of the sacrifice	*Panchavimsa* *Taittiriya*	Gradual Compilation
	The Aryans in the Middle Land	*Talavakara*	of the *Atharvaveda*
Isaiah, the Prophet, 737-700 B.C.	Writing introduced	*Kauskitaki* *Aitareya* *Satapatha*	
	Rise of the Vanaprasthas	*Gopatha*	

Atharva-veda

During this period a fourth Veda, the *Atharvaveda,* was compiled. Although as a collection it is later than the other three, a great deal of the material embodied in it is of early date. It is a more popular work than the other Vedas, reflecting the superstitions of the people, and consists mostly of charms, which are of two classes, those that bring weal and those that bring woe. It was some time before the *Atharvaveda* received equal recognition with the the older collections.

A Charm against Fever

Hence, filled with holy strength let Agni, Soma, and Varuna, the Press-stone, and the Altar,
And Grass, and glowing Fuel banish Fever. Let hateful things stay at a distance yonder.
And thou thyself who makest all men yellow, consuming them with burning heat like Agni,

Thou, Fever! then be weak and ineffective. Pass hence into the realms below or vanish.

Go, Fever, to the Mujavats, or farther, to the Bahlikas. Seek a lascivious Sudra girl and seem to shake her through and through.

Go hence and eat thy kinsmen the Mahavrishas and Mujavats.

These or those foreign regions we proclaim to Fever for his home.

Go Fever, with Consumption, thy brother, and with thy sister, Cough,

And with thy nephew Herpes, go away unto that alien folk.

Chase Fever whether cold or hot, brought by the summer or the rains,

Tertian, intermittent, or autumnal, or continual.

We to Gandharis, Mujavats, to Angas and to Magadhas

Hand over Fever as it were a servant and a thing of price.

—*Atharvaveda,* V. xxii.

Philosophic Period

Karma and Rebirth

तद्यदेतदिदम्मयोऽदोमय इति
यथाकारी यथाचारी तथा भवति।

'In proportion as a man consists now of this or that, just as he acts, just as he behaves, so will he be born.'

—*Brihadaranyaka Upanishad, IV. iv.*

(The text is one of the earliest utterances on Karma and Rebirth.)

History. This period saw the completion of the spread of Aryan influence all over North India, and the still further progress of the organisation of the people under the Brahmins. North India was divided into a large number of different states, of which a few were ruled as republics, but the majority as monarchies. Several of them were of considerable size, and had great military power. The chief of them were undoubtedly Magadha, corresponding roughly to Bihar, and Kosala, corresponding roughly to Oudh. The capitals of these states were now large, prosperous, wealthy cities. Industry, trade, and the simple arts were progressing. A rude coinage, consisting of rectangular pieces of gold, silver, and copper, with a few signs punched on them, was introduced. There were still vast tracts of country under forest, but each of the states contained scenes of busy, happy life; and there was constant communication between all the chief points.

Religion. During this period the Brahmins continued their sacrificial work, and also carried on the great task of bringing the aborigines under the influence of Aryan culture. New gods and demigods constantly found their way into the pantheon. The schools of the priests were more important than ever. The city of Taxila in the extreme north-west of the Punjab was the chief centre of learning.

Religion as a whole remained much as it was during the previous period. Innumerable sacrifices were still offered, and the old beliefs continued unchanged for most people. **But the more intelligent men underwent a revolutionary change.**

(a) The old hazy pantheistic faith became clear and was grasped more firmly. The whole world was paltry and unreal in comparison with the One which informed it and was its sole Reality. All the ordinary gods were spoken of as mere temporary manifestations of the unchanging and actionless Absolute. Yet the worship of the gods went on unchanged, as the Absolute is unknowable.

THE ONE REALITY

Who is he whom we meditate on as the self? What is that self? That by which one sees, by which one hears, by which one smells scents, by which one forms speech, by which one discriminates sweet and sour? That which is the heart and the mind, perception, injunction, understanding, knowledge, wisdom, vision, firmness, thinking, considering, helping, memory, resolution, will, breath, love, and desire? All these are only names of knowledge. That self is *brahman,* Indra, Prajapati, all the gods, the five great elements, earth, air, ether, water, lights, all these and those which are mixed with small as it were, seeds of various minds, born of eggs, born from the womb, born from heat, born from germs, horses, cows, men, elephants, and all that breathes, whether it walks or flies, and what is immovable. All that is guided by knowledge, it rests on knowledge. The world is guided by knowledge. Knowledge is its foundation. Knowledge is *brahman.* He by his knowing self, having left this world and having obtained all delights in the world of heaven, became immortal.

—*Aitareya Aranyaka,* ii. 6.

(b) The problems raised by the varying fortunes of men and the extraordinary differences in character met with everywhere were solved for the Indian mind by the doctrine of Transmigration and its pendant Karma.

The doctrine of Transmigration is that souls are emanations of the divine spirit, sparks from the central fire, drops from the ocean of divinity, that each soul is incarnated in a body times without number, that the same soul may be in one life a god, in another a man, in a third an animal or even a plant, and that there can be no rest for the soul, no relief from suffering until it finds release from the necessity of birth and returns to the divine source whence it came.

The word Karma means literally action, but the doctrine means the inevitable working out of action in new life. The idea is that a man's body, character, capacities and temperament, his birth, wealth and station, and the whole of his experience in life, whether of happiness or of sorrow, together form the just retribution for his deeds, good and bad, done in earlier existences. The expiation works itself out not only in his passive experience *(bhoktritvam),* but in his actions also *(kartritvam).* Then these new actions form new karma which must necessarily be expiated in another existence; so that, as fast as the clock of retribution runs down, it winds itself up again.

Release or Salvation

(c) As it is deeds, good or bad, that form karma, and thus lead to rebirth, the idea lies ready to hand that, if by any means a man can cease acting, he may thereby get Release (liberation or salvation) from the necessity of rebirth. Quite naturally and unreflectingly men took action to mean the business of life; so there arose the universal conviction that, if a man wished to reach Release, he must give up the ordinary life of man with all its gains, pleasures and interests and live an actionless existence, turning away from the unreal world and drawing near the one actionless Reality. The ascetic is the only truly religious man, according to this doctrine.

(d) It was perhaps the doctrine of the frequent rebirth of souls which suggested the theory of the cyclic destruction and recreation of the world. The idea is that the crude, external, phenomenal world periodically returns to a state of undifferentiated invisibility; souls leave their bodies; and matter and souls remain in undisturbed peace until the moment comes for a new creation. Then matter begins once more to evolve; inorganic things, the vegetable world, animals, men and gods come into being; the process of transmigration begins at the precise point where it stopped when the world disappeared; the castes are re-formed; the *rishis* see the Vedas once more; and thus the world comes to be just as it was before.

Kalpa

The period between creation and destruction is called a *kalpa,* the period of repose a *pralaya.* So much is common to all schools of Hindus, and to Buddhists as well. In the subdivision of the *kalpa* a descending series of four ages, corresponding roughly to the golden, silver, bronze, and iron ages of the Classics, is much used, but there are considerable differences in the detailed application of the idea. The Jains drop out the period of repose, and divide time into alternating periods of degeneration and progress. In all schools time has neither beginning nor end.

The Ages of the World

There is some reason for thinking that at first the following was the whole scheme of the *Kalpa:*

Kritayuga
Treta yuga
Dvapara yuga = *Kalpa*
Kali yuga

The names are taken from the game of dice, *Krita,* 'the four', designating the Golden Age, when virtue is four-square; *Treta,* 'the three', designating the Silver Age, when one-fourth part of virtue has been lost; *Dvapara,* 'the two', when one-half of virtue has disappeared; and *Kali,* 'the one', when only one-fourth part of good remains. *Yuga* is the Sanskrit word for 'age'.

But the scheme was much elaborated by the various schools; and the doctrine finally adopted by orthodox Hinduism is that these four ages make one *Mahayuga* or

Great Age, and that it takes 1,000 *Mahayugas* to complete a *Kalpa*.

The number of dice spots was applied also to the length of the ages as under:

Dawn 400 Day 4,000 Twilight 400	= *Krila yuga*	
Dawn 300 Day 3,000 Twilight 300	= *Treta yuga*	
Dawn 200 Day 2,000 Twilight 200	= *Dvapara yuga*	= *Mahayuga*
Dawn 100 Day 1,000 Twilight 100.	= *Kali yuga*	

This elaborate scheme arose much later than the philosophic period.

(e) The Brahmin was everywhere accepted as the divine teacher and sacrificer; his Veda was the one Revelation and Caste was the heaven-sent system for the social organisation of the people.

Essential Hinduism

(f) This then is essential Hinduism:

A. *The Theory of God and the world,* consisting of

1. The one impersonal Reality and the unreal phenomenal world, which undergoes cyclic change. All minor gods are gathered under the pantheistic All.
2. Transmigration and Karma the explanation of the world.
3. Release from Transmigration and union with the one Reality, the object of all serious men.

B. The organisating conception, consisting of

1. The divine priest
2. The inspired Veda
3. Caste

(g) By the time that this new conception of the world had taken distinct form, it had become the custom to send every boy belonging to the Brahmin, Kshatriya, and Vaisya castes to a Brahminical school to receive an education. A ceremony of initiation introduced the lad to this religious training. A Brahmin priest muttered sacred texts over him and put the sacred thread on his shoulder; and immediately the reafter his education began. It was a birth into a new life. Hence these three castes are known as twice-born. The fact that every man of these castes spent several years under Brahmin discipline and teaching explains in some degree the extraordinary influence of the priestly class. No one but a Brahmin was allowed to teach. Teaching, sacrificing, and receiving gifts were the three functions which belonged to them by virtue of their birth. This universal education of the boys of the three twice-born castes, coupled with the absolute exclusion of every other one from this, the one avenue to culture and knowledge then open in India, helps to explain the great predominance of these castes throughout India. No arrangement was made for giving girls an education; marriage took the place of initiation in their case.

(h) By the end of our period we have trustworthy evidence to prove that two of the most characteristic Hindu customs were regarded as right, namely, the use of idols in worship and child-marriage. The Hindu law enjoined that a girl should be married before she reached the age of puberty and this necessarily led to child-marriage. We may also note that by this time only the childless widow was allowed to re-marry.

प्रदानं प्रागृतोः ।।

'A girl should be given in marriage before puberty.'

—*Gautama, Dharmasutra, xviii.* 21.

This brief outline of Essential Hinduism is sufficient to show us what an overturning change the Indian mind had experienced. The steadily growing culture of the Brahmins and the wider experience of men and things which they were daily acquiring as they went on with the work of reducing the whole population of India under their own religious sway had brought them to this new and far-reaching system of thought. **Under the wide dome of this universal pantheism they were able to gather all the aboriginal worships of the land and by tactful arrangements to give them a certain distinct unity.** The common people continued their worship practically unchanged: only Brahmin teachers taught Transmigration everywhere, and spoke of the great God behind all gods. How different all this is from the beliefs of the *Rigveda* !

This radical system has been taught wherever Hinduism has gone; it lies behind all the philosophies and is implied in the asceticism, the laws, the worship, and the life of the people.

THE UPANISHADS

असतो मा सद्गमय
तमसो मा ज्योतिर्गमय
मृत्योर्माऽमृतं गमय ।।

From the unreal lead me to the real!
From darkness lead me to light!
From death lead me to immortality!

—*Brihadaranyaka Upanishad,* 1. iii. 28.

A time came when **there arose a great passion among thinking men in North India to win Release, and many**

theories as to the true path to Emancipation were proclaimed. Most of the leaders declared that Release was the fruit of knowledge, but others laid stress on sacrifice or Vedic study, and many declared that the true means was *tapas,* austerity. So, many went out to the old hermitages and sought by self-torture to reach the end of birth and sorrow.

But the more serious men went farther. They regarded the whole phenomenal world as inherently antagonistic to the spiritual life. They therefore decided to go much farther than the hermits: they gave up the worship of the gods, ancestor-worship and all family connexions, and became homeless. They might seek Release either by *tapas,* or by knowledge, or by a combination of the two; but in any case they abandoned all connexion with the life of men. This new type of ascetic was called *parivrajaka,* wanderer; *bhikshu,* beggar; *sannyasi,* renouncer.

The attempt to reach Release by means of true knowledge led to momentous results. **Many theories of the constitution of the world were formed and taught; but the most important of all is the doctrine of the Upanishads.** The ordinary name for the World-soul was *Brahman,* a neuter noun which expresses the common thought of the time, that the World-soul is an impersonal essence present in all things. There were many speculations as to its nature; until some wise thinker called Brahman the *atman,* or Self of the universe. Then, as the soul of the universe was *atman,* and the soul of the individual was *atman,* the conclusion was soon drawn that the two were identical. The great affirmation was made, 'My self is the infinite self'; 'the soul of the universe, whole and undivided, dwells in me.' Thus self-knowledge is knowledge of God; and, as knowledge of God leads to Release, the man who realises the identity of his soul with the World-soul is thereby set free from the cycle of births and deaths; he will not be born again. The great phrases used are. **'Thou art That,' 'I am Brahman,' and 'I am He.' This is the Vedanta philosophy in its earliest form.**

The Identity of the Human and the Divine Self

'Place this salt in water, and then wait on me in the morning.'

The son did as he was commanded.

The father said to him: 'Bring me the salt, which you placed in the water last night.'

The son, having looked for it, found it not, for, of course, it was melted.

The father said: 'Taste it from the surface of the water. How is it?'

The son replied: 'It is salt.'

'Taste it from the middle. How is it?'

The son replied: 'It is salt.'

'Taste it from the bottom. How is it?'

The son replied: 'It is salt.'

The father said: 'Throw it away and then wait on me.' He did so; but salt exists for ever.

Then the father said: 'Here also, in this body, forsooth, you do not perceive the True, my son; but there indeed it is. That which is the subtle essence, in it all that exists has its self. That is the True. That is 1he Self, and thou, O Svetaketu, art That.'

—*Chhandogya Upanishad,* vi. 13;

The conception of Brahman-Atman in the Upanishads is a great lightning-flash of truth, and it is placed before us in many a noble passage: Brahman is Consciousness: Brahman is the Reality of everything; Brahman is joy; Brahman is incomprehensible; by the command of Brahman all things are done. The phrase, *sachchidananda Brahma,* 'Brahman is reality, intelligence, and bliss,' is a very late one, not found in this period at all, but it sums up Upanishad thought with great accuracy.

सत्यं ज्ञानमनन्तं ब्रह्म यो वेद
सोऽश्नुतं सर्वान् कामान्।।

'He who knows Brahman as Reality, Knowledge, Eternal, he obtains all desires.'

—*Taittiriya Upanishad,* II. i. I.

The philosophy of the Atman sketched above was by means the only philosophic system put forward as the way to Release. Numerous philosophic leaders stand out dimly in the pale historic light, each with his own specialised doctrine and his following of monks. In an old Buddhist book **there is a catalogue of sixty-two different theories of the universe taught at this time in North India.** All these system-builders had a great deal in common. Transmigration was accepted as an axiom, and also the beliefs, that earthly things had to be given up if Release was to be won, and that knowledge was the right means of Release. Hence the search for knowledge and the wandering monkish life were universal among philosophers. Women also adopted the wandering life; so that each school had nuns as well as monks.

It seems to be certain that the Sankhya system as well as the Vedanta was sketched at this early date, but no treatise of the school belonging to this period survives. Among the numerous teachers of the time two stand out above all others, Mahavira, the Jain leader, and Gautama, the founder of Buddhism. They were contemporaries,

Mahavīra the older of the two. It seems that Gautama's death occurred within a few years of 480 B.C., the date which closes our period.

Jainism

Jainism was originally merely a specialisation and intensification of the old ascetic discipline under the influence of an extreme reverence for life and of a belief that not only men, animals, and plants, but the smallest particles of earth, fire, water, and wind are endowed with living souls. Consequently, a very large part of the Jain monk's attention was directed to using the extremest care not to injure any living thing. So eager were the Jains to part with the world to the uttermost that many of their monks wore not a scrap of clothing. Twelve years of most severe asceticism were necessary for salvation. After that, if a monk did not wish to live longer, he was recommended to starve himself to death.

Buddhism

Buddhism, on the other hand, while it recommended a mild asceticism, condemned self-torture, and found salvation in *knowledge* and *right living.* The knowledge which Buddha taught was summed up by him in three propositions, known as 'the three characteristics of being', namely:

All its constituents are transitory;
All its constituents are misery;
All its constituents are lacking in an ego.

If a man realised that all things are fleeting, that life is sorrow, and that he has no soul to save, he will thereby be set free from the chains of the world, and will experience the *nirvana* (extinction) of lust, hatred, and ignorance. Having reached freedom, he will live his life according to the noble laws of Buddha. Being thus a conqueror over the world, he will at death enter final *nirvana;* he will not be born again.

No God

Buddhism, Jainism, and the Sankhya system do not teach the existence of the living eternal only God, but they recognise all the godlings of the Hindu system, giving them humble place.

Philosophic leaders in those days received numerous honorific titles from their followers, *buddha* (enlightened), *jina* (conqueror), *tirthakara* (ford-maker, i.e., religious leader), etc. Gautama finally became known as the Buddha, Mahavira as the Jina (whence the word Jain).

Both of these leaders also formed an outer circle of lay followers, who were not required to practise the asceticism of the monks, but obeyed easy regulations.

Literature etc. The Brahmins, perceiving the power of the philosophy of the Atman, were not slow to adopt it and to introduce it into their schools. There it was taught as a special discipline preparatory to the life of the *parivrajaka,* while ordinary Brahmin pupils took it as an extra subject at the close of the regular priestly course. As this knowledge was regarded as the final aim of all Veda study, it was called *Vedanta,* i.e., Veda-end.

Gradually the allegorical teaching given as a preparation for the hermit life, and the philosophic instruction intended for the wandering life, took definite shape and were handed down orally from teacher to pupil in fixed language, each school having its own sacred deposit. The former was called *aranyaka,* or 'forest teaching', as we have seen; the latter *upanishad,* probably in the sense of 'secret doctrine '. Thus were formed the wonderful treatises which we know as the Aranyakas and the Upanishads. It is to be noted that the two types of teaching frequently overlap in one document.

To this early period belong only the first great group of prose treatises, written in the style of the Brahmanas, the four Aranyakas and the *Brihadaranyaka, Chhandogya, Taittiriya, Aitareya, Kaushitaki,* and *Kena* Upanishads. These have been used devotionally all through the centuries by a small but select company of intellectual and spiritual men.

THE RELATIVE AGE OF THE EARLY UPANISHADS

Events outside India	*History*	*Religion*	*Literature*
Zoroaster, 660-583 B.C. The *Avesta*	All North India under Aryan influence	Transmigration and Karma accepted	The early prose Upanishads
Jeremiah. 627-580 B.C.	Rise of great cities		1. *Brihadaranyaka*
		Taxila a seat of learning	2. *Chhandogya*
	Coinage appears		
		Idols in Hinduism	3. *Taittiriya*
Pythagoras, died about 510 B.C.	Gradual Conquest of the South		4. *Aitareya*
Athens a republic, 510 B.C.Rome a republic, 509 B.C.		Rise of Jainism Rise of Buddhism	5. *Kaushitaki* 6. *Kena*
		Death of Mahavira	
Confucius the Chinese sage, 551-479 B. c.	Darius conquers the Punjab 500 B.C.	Death of Gautama about 480 B.C.	*The Ramayana,* II-VI

During this period the theory that the Brahmanas with their appendices, the Aranyakas and the Upanishads, are Revelation, *sruti,* in precisely the same sense as the Vedas themselves, took shape and found acceptance. Indeed it became customary to use the word Veda to cover all this prose literature as well as the hymns; so that one has constantly to ask whether the word is used in the wide or the narrow sense. The theory was that no hymn or Brahmana had a human author, but that they were eternal, and that they had been seen by the *rishis,* i.e., 'seers'. Through this idea the limits of the canon were fixed. All that is *sruti* is included; all that is not *sruti* is excluded.

Sruti, the Hindu Canon

Many later Upanishads, not included in this table, are recognized as *sruti* also; they have no definite place in any Vedic school, but are loosely attached to the *Atharvaveda,*

Veda	*Brahmana for the Priest*	*Aranyaka for the Hermit*	*Upanishad for the Wanderer*
Rik	1. *Aitareya*	1. *Aitareya*	1. *Aitareya*
	2. *Kaushitaki*	2. *Kaushitaki*	2. *Kaushitaki*
Saman	I. *Pancha-vimsa*		
	2. *(Chhndo-gya)*		2. *Chhandogya,*
	3. *Talavakara*		3. *Kena*
Black Yajus	1. *Taittiriya*	1. *Taittiriya*	1. *Taittiriya Mahanarayana*
	2.		2. *Kathaka*
	3.		3. *Maitrayaniya Svetasvatara*
While Yajus	1. *Satapatha*	1. *Brihat*	1. *Brihadaranyaka Isa*
Atharvan	*Gopatha*		*Mundaka*
			Prasna
			Mandukya

The Veda was held to be so sacred that to reveal any portion of it to anyone other than a member of the three highest castes was regarded as a sin. There is a vast amount of sacred literature besides this, but it is only *smriti,* 'recollection', that is Tradition. It has only a limited authority.

Towards the end of this period the *Ramayana* in its earliest form, which consisted of only five books (ii-vi), was composed by Valmiki, in the kingdom of Kosala. In this work Rama is a purely human hero.

SUTRAS AND SUTTAS

BUDDHAM SARANAM GACCHAMI
DHAMMAM SARANAM GACCHAMI
SANGHAM SARANAM GACCHAMI

The formula of entrance into Buddhism. 'I take refuge in the Buddha; I take refuge in the Doctrine; I take refuge in the Order.'

History. The greatest fact to be realised with regard to the history of this period is the gradual Aryanising of South India. We have no detailed account of how it was carried out. Doubtless the chief work was done by Brahmin priests, who went all over the south country as missionarIes of the faith and civilisation of their people, but Aryan warriors also won themselves kingdoms in the south.

Darius conquered the basin of the Indus. and a part of the Punjab about 500 B.C., but we do not know how long Persian rule lasted there. Apart from this, North India remained practically as it was before until 321 B.C. The literature speaks of the existence of sixteen leading powers in North India in these centuries. The invasion of the Punjab by Alexander in 326 B.C. did not disturb appreciably the other parts of India; and very soon after his death in 323 B.C. a revolt destroyed the Greek power in the Punjab.

HINDU IDOLS

The earliest surviving representations of Hindu idols occur in Buddhist sculpture. This is the goddess Sri from the Bharhut Stupa, now in Calcutta Museum.

But the young adventurer who overthrew the Greeks in the Punjab soon brought the whole of the northern half of India under his rule, and thus founded the first empire ever known in India (321 B.C.). His name was Chandragupta, and Pataliputra, i.e., Patna, the capital of Magadha, was his capital. His grandson, **Asoka (272-231 B.C.)**, ruied a large part of South India also. **Under this man, a ruler of the highest capacity and character, civilisation made great strides.** Stone architecture and sculpture made their appearance in India during his reign, and from his time onwards inscriptions are common. His descendants, however, proved unfit for imperial power; and the empire gradually weakened and finally broke up in 184 B.C. After Alexander the coinage of India became artistic under the influence of the mints of Greece, Bactria, and Persia.

Religion. During this period Hinduism with its Veda and caste-system, its priests and regulated worship, completed the conquest of the peninsula. From this time onwards the Brahmins are everywhere recognised as divine representatives of the gods. But, although they became supreme wherever they went, and brought the better part of the population under their care, there were large sections of the people everywhere whom they considered low and degraded to receive their ministrations. The descendants of these groups are found to this day in all parts of the country.

This period is scholastic in most of its religious features. Hindu practice became steadily more regular under the unceasing pressure of priestly authority. This is most noteworthy in the realm of social life: at the beginning of the period there was still a considerable amount of caste laxity throughout Norhten India, but by the close a great advance had taken place. The whole system had hardened

A HINDU TEMPLE IN BUDDHIST SCULPTURE

From the Sanchi Stupa of second century B.C. The divinity is a five-handed snake, or Naga, which is visible within the shrine. In front stands a fire-altar, while a Vanaprastha and his leafy hut may be seen in the right foreground.

and was very much what it has been for centuries. A large number of the secondary castes were already in existence.

One of the chief characteristics of the priesthood at this time was the desire to express everything with great exactness in well-arranged manuals, each devoted to a single subject. This scholastic tendency comes out very distinctly in Buddhist literature also; everything is classified, arranged in groups, numbered and labelled. There are four Noble Truths; the Noble Path is eight-fold; there are twelve steps in the theory of Dependent Origination, the Buddhist theory of how living beings come into existence. The same is true of Jainism.

Temples

Images and temples rose during this period to the place which they have ever since held in Hindu life. The traditional appearance of the various gods, with their dress, weapons, and ornaments, became definitely fixed; while the plan of the temple court was modelled on the arrangements of the ground for the ancient sacrifices.

When Gautama the Buddha died, his relics, divided into seven portions, were laid in seven stupas erected for them; and the great teachers who followed him were similarly honoured. Nor was that all. Buddhists soon began to believe that the truth had been taught by a long sucression of Buddhas before Gautama, and that in the next age another, named Maitreya, would arise. All these things stirred feelings of piety and reverence in Buddhist hearts. Crowds of lay believers bowed down before the great stupas in reverent meditation, adoring the relics and repeating sacred formulas, and walked round the stupas in solemn religious march. To these observances and to the stated gatherings

NORTH GATE OF THE SANCHI STUPA

This noble monument stands at Sanchi. The huge mound of the stupa is visible behind the gate, but the ornament on the top is gone. Portions of the stone rail are visible on each side of the gate. There are three other gates.

in the *chaityas,* or assembly halls, we must attribute the beginnings of Buddhist worship.

King Asoka

In the ninth year of his reign Asoka became a Buddhist layman. Later he actually became a monk. He spent a great deal of energy in trying to lead his subjects to the adoption of the moral teaching of Buddhism. For this purpose, he had long edicts cut on rocks in various parts of his empire, calling on the people to cultivate filial piety, righteousness, reverence for all religions, and kindness to animals. He elected hospitals for man and beast, and in every way sought the welfare of his subjects. Innumerable religious edifices were erected to his order, chiefly stupas, chaityas, monasteries, and rock-cut cells for monks. **But the most significant act of his reign was the sending out of missionaries to spread Buddhism throughout India and the neighbouring lands.** As a result Ceylon became a Buddhist country, and the religion also made great progress beyond the river Indus and upon the Himalayas. It was Asoka that made Buddhism a world-conquering power.

The first beginnings of worship among the Jains appeared in much the same way as they did in Buddhism; but this community was not so successful at this time in securing royal and wealthy patrons as the Buddhists were. Their earliest monuments are two to three centuries later.

Then the Jain community broke in two in A.D. 82. It was a question of clothes that led to the separation. The monks of one section wore no clothing and were, therefore, called *Digambara,* 'clothed-in-atmosphere', while the monks of the other group wore white robes and were called *Svetambara,* 'clothed-in-white'.

BUDDHIST WORSHIP

Men and angels adoring a stupa. A relief from the rail of the Bharhut Stupa of the second century B.C.

Literature. Quite early in this period, the earliest form of the great epic, the *Mahabharata,* appeared. It probably arose in the country between the Ganges and the Jumna. It was then a poem of very moderate length, containing about 8,800 couplets and was called the *Bharata.* Krishna is a purely human hero in it.

Satyaki's Sons Slain

Morning with her fiery radiance oped the portals of the day,
Shone once more on Kuru warriors, Pandav chiefs in dread array!

Bhima and the gallant Arjun led once more the van of war,

But the proud preceptor Drona faced them in his sounding car!

Still with gallant son of Arjun, Lakshman strove with bow and shield,

Vainly strove; his faithful henchman bore him bleeding from the field!

Lakshman, son of proud Duryodhan! Abhimanyu, Arjun's son!

Doomed to die in youth and glory 'neath the same revolving sun!

Sad the day for Vrishni warriors! Brave Satyaki's sons of might,

'Gainst the cruel Bhurisravas strove in unrelenting fight,

Ten brave brothers, pride of Vrishni, fell upon that fatal day,

Slain by mighty Bhurisravas, and upon the red field lay!

—*Mahabharata*

BUDDHIST WORSHIP

A *chaitya* or Buddhist hall and Buddhists adoring a *dharmachakra,* or wheel of the doctrine, a symbol of Buddha's teaching. A relief from the Bharhut Stupa.

The teaching of each philosophic leader was handed down orally in his monastic school. It is noteworthy, however, that Sanskrit was used in the Brahminic schools, while the Jains and the Buddhists used the vernaculars.

As knowledge grew and the compass and the number of the subjects taught in the Brahminical schools went on increasing, the mass of material to be learned by rote became more and more unmanageable. It became impossible for the student to store in his memory everything which he wanted to know, so long as it was presented to him in the extraordinarily prolix manner of the Brahmins. A new method was therefore invented. All the knowledge which the student had to acquire was expressed in strings of aphorisms of the briefest and most pregnant description. As time went on and the new method developed, it became a conventional system of technical terms like a modern telegraphic code. These tabloids of condensed knowledge were called *sutras*. Is not this the very climax of scholasticism?

Sutras

A literal translation of each sutra is given in italics, and then the meaning follows in roman.

Now, therefore, the right.

Now, therefore, the right of performing sacrificial acts will be laid down here.

Acts fruit-attended.

Sacrificial acts are attended by fruits, such as heaven, wealth, etc.

Of all without distinction.

One would expect that there must be a right of all living beings without distinction to perform sacrificial acts; as all desire fruits.

But of human beings from the power of undertaking.

But the right belongs to human beings only, because they only have the power of undertaking sacrificial acts.

Cripple, ignorant, eunuch, Sudra except.

Cripples, those ignorant of the Veda, eunuchs, Sudras are to the excepted.

Of Brahmins, Rajanyas, Vaisyas, from sruti.

The right belongs to Brahmins, Kshatriyas and Vaisyas, but not to Sudras, according to Vedic precept.

A woman also without distinction.

A woman also has the right, as there is no distinction between her and her husband.

—Katyayana, *Srauta Sutra,* i. 1-7.

These books, if books they can be called when they were not written down, dealt with all the subjects of a priest's education. They were usually summed up under six heads, called the *vedangas,* or members of the body of the Veda.

शिक्षा कल्पो व्याकरणं
निरुक्तं छन्दो ज्योतिषं ।।

THE SIX VEDANGAS:—*siksha,* pronunciation; *kalpa,* ceremonial; *vyakarana,* grammar; *nirukta,* etymology; *chhandas,* metre; *jyotisha,* astronomy.

Of the six, Kalpa, ceremonial, is the most important. Under Kalpa there are three groups of *sutras,* the *Srauta Sutras,* which deal with the sacrifices, summarising the teaching of the Brahmanas, the *Grihya Sutras,* which deal with domestic ceremonies, and the *Dharma Sutras,* which provide rules of conduct for the various classes of men and the various stages of life. The Brahminical schools were now more numerous than ever, many of the earlier schools having split into several branches; and each had its own series of *sutras,* dealing in turn with all the subjects comprehended under the six *vedangas.* Panini, the great grammarian, wrote in *sutras,* and his work comes under *vyakarana,* one of the *vedangas.* He was connected with Taxila and flourished about 300 B.C.

SCHOLASTIC PERIOD 480 TO 184 B.C.

Sutras are the characteristic type of Hindu literature throughout this period, The *Gautama Dharmasutra,* whIch is the earliest of the Dharma class, probably dates from the end of the philosophic period, and one or two of the Srauta class may be as early. In any case, all three classes, Srauta, Grihya and Dharma, continued to be composed thoughout the period. They are not set down in this table, because their chronological order is not yet known.

External events	*History*	*Religion*	*Literature*	
	Continued conquest of the South		VERSE UPANISHADS	Earliest form of the *Mahabharata*
400			*Kathaka*	
Socrates drinks the hemlock, 399 B.C. Plato, 427-347 Aristotle, 384-322			*Isa*	

The Avesta burned by Alexander 300	Alexander in the Punjab		*Svetasvatara*	Gradual Formation of of the Buddhist Pali Canon, the Tripitaka
	Asoka	Rise of Buddhist architecture Buddhist missionaries sent out by Asoka	*Mundaka*	
200			*Mahanarayana*	
184	Fall of Asokan Empire			

Chief Manuals of the Vedic Schools

This table is meant to show at a glance the way in which the Vedic literature grew up, and to which school each great manual belongs. The numbers show the school connexion: thus the great Taittiriya school of the Black Yajur Veda had a full series of manuals, Brahmana, Aranyaka, Upanishad, Srauta, Grihya, and Dharma sutras. Brackets are used to keep together the branch schools belonging to each ancient *charana*. Where there is uncertainty about the school to which a manual belongs, no number is prefixed to the name, as in the case of the *Vasishtha Dharmasutra.* One *Dharmasutra* has been put in brackets: the reason is that no manuscript of it has been found; it is known only by quotation; but it is mentioned, because it is the source whence the *Manava Dharmasastra* sprang. All this literature was taught only by Brahmins and only to men of the three twiceborn castes. Women and men of other castes were not allowed to hear it.

Sruti			
Veda	*Brahmana*	*Aranyaka*	*Upanishad*
RIK	1. *Aitareya*	1. *Aitareya*	1. *Aitareya*
	2. *Kaushitaki*	2. *Kaushtaki*	2. *Kaushitaki*
SAMAN	1. Panchavimsa		
	2. (*Chhandogya*)	2. *Chhandogya*	
	3. *Talavakara*		3. *Kena*
BLACK	1. *Taittiriya*	1. *Taittiriya*	1. *Taittiriya*
VAJUS	2.		*Mahanarayana*
	3.		
WHITE YAJUS	1. *Satapatha*	1. *Brihat*	1. *Brihadaran-aka*
ATHARVAN	*Gopatha*		*Mundaka* *Prasna* *Mandukya*

Smriti

Srauta Sutra	*Grihya Sutra*	*Dharma Sutra*
1. *Asvalayana*	1. *Asvalayana*	*Vasishtha*
2. *Sankhayana*	2. *Sankhayana.* *Sambavya*	
1. *Masaka* *Drahyayana* *Latyayana*	1. *Gobhila* *Khadira*	1. *Gautama*
1. *Baudhayana* *Apastamba* *Hiranyakesin* *Bharadvaja*	1. *Baudhayana* *Apastamba* *Hiranyakesin* *Bharadvaja*	1. *Baudhayana* *Apastamba* *Hiranyakesin*
	2. *Kathaka*	
3. *Manava*	3. *Manava*	(3. *Manava)*
1. *Katyayana*	1. *Paraskara*	
Vaitana		
Kausika	*Kausika*	

Interrelations of Vedic Literature

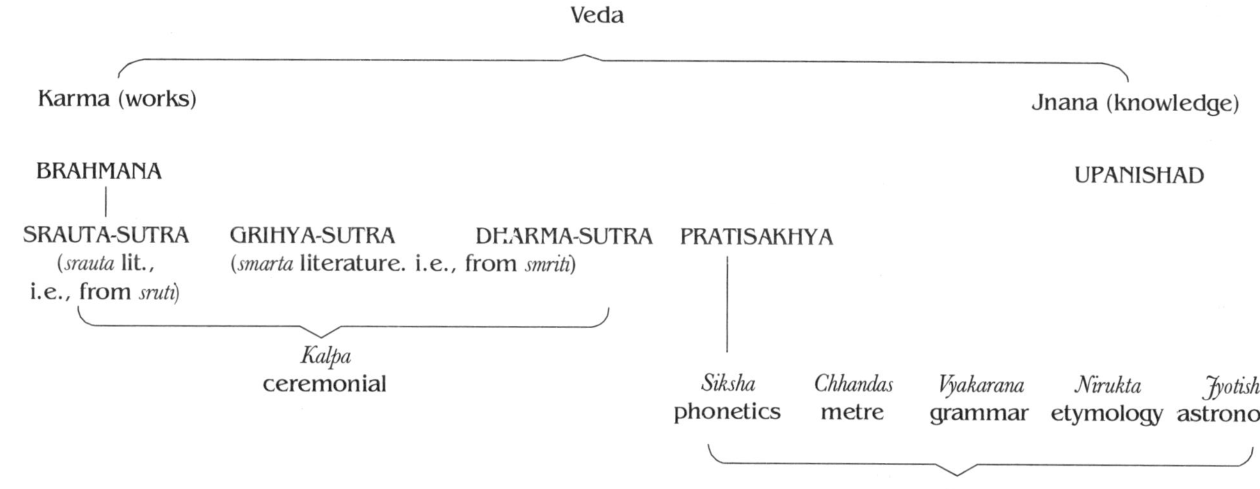

The Four Asramas

During the scholastic period, it was recognsied that the ideal life for a Brahmin was to spend twelve years as a student, then to marry and beget children, and then to retire to the forest as a hermit, taking his wife with him, if he chose to do so.

At a still later date a fourth stage was added: the Brahmin was recommended, after he had lived as a hermit, to end his days as a houseless *parivrajaka,* thinking only of God.

1. *Brahmachari:* student.
2. *Grihastha:* householder.
3. *Vanaprastha:* forest-dweller, hermit.
4. *Parivrajaka:* wanderer, houseless monk.

The language used in the Brahminical schools was gradually polished and brought under phonetic and grammatical rules, while, with the spread of the people all over North India, the ordinary language had necessarily developed into a number of provincial vernaculars. The literary tongue of the schools was called *samskrita;* i.e., polished, while the vernaculars were called *prakrita,* i.e., natural. Panini's grammar finally fixed the form of Sanskrit. Already in his day it was very distinct from the popular dialects. These latter naturally continued to change, and they have produced the great modern Aryan languages of India, Hindi, Punjabi, Gujarati, Marathi, Bengali, Oriya, Assamese, and the rest.

In certain of the schools at this time some of the best parts of the old Upanishads were versified and strung together, so as to make new Upanishads. The brief, pointed, aphoristic character of these poems shows plainly that they were put together with a view to their easily committed to memory.

A Passage from a Verse Upanishad

As the one fire that passed into the world
Has there transformed itself to many forms,
So the one Self within all creatures
Transforms itself to many forms, while outside all.

As the one air that passed into the world
Has there transformed itself to many forms,
So the one Self within all creatures
Transforms itself to many forms, while outside all.

Just as the sun, the whole world's eye,
By visible external foulness ne'er is tainted,
So the one Self within all creatures
By the world's sorrow ne'er is tainted, being outside it.

The one Controller, the Self within all creatures,
Who makes the one form manifold
Those wise men who behold Him in the self,
They and no others have eternal joy.

He who, Eternal, Conscious, One, fulfils
The longings of the Transient, Conscious, Many—
Those wise men who behold Him in the self,
They and no others have eternal peace.

The truth, that this is That, they feel to be
Bliss indescribable, supreme.
How can I come to know it?
Shines it effulgent, or reflecting light?

There shineth not the sun, nor moon and stars;
These lightnings shine not; how much less this fire!
His lonely shining makes the All resplendent!
'Tis with His glory that this whole world gleams!

—*Kathaka Upanishad,* v.

As we have seen, the Jains and the Buddhists used not Sanskrit, but the vernaculars in teaching their hearers. Their sermons were called *suttas,* which is the vernacular form of the Sanskrit *sutras.* These were handed down by word of mouth from teacher to pupil; but during the earliest generations they were considerably changed and expanded.

A Buddhist Sutta

Thus have I heard.

On a certain occasion The Blessed One was dwelling at Savatthi in Jetavana monastery in Anathapindika's Park.

And there The Blessed One addressed the monks.

'Monks,' said he.

'Lord,' said the monks to The Blessed One in reply. And The Blessed One spoke as follows:

'I will teach you, O monks, the burden, the bearer of the burden, the taking up of the burden, and the laying down of the burden.

'And what, O monks, is the burden?

'Reply should be made that it is the five attachment groups. And what are the five? They are: the form attachment-group, the sensation-attachment-group, the perception-attachment-group, the predisposition-attachment-group, the consciousness-attachment-group. These, O monks, are called the burden.

'And who, O monks, is the bearer of the burden?

'Reply should be made that it is the individual; the venerable So-and-so of such-and-such a family. He, O monks, is called the bearer of the burden.

'And what, O monks, is the taking up of the burden?

'It is desire leading to rebirth, joining itself to pleasure and passion, and finding delight in every existence-desire, namely, for sensual pleasure, desire for permanent existence, desire for transitory existence. This, O monks, is called the taking up of the burden.

'And what, O monks, is the laying down of the burden?

'It is the complete absence of passion, the cessation, giving up, relinquishment, forsaking, and non-adoption of desire. This, O monks, is called the laying down of the burden.'

—*Samyutta-Nikaya*, xxii. 22, I

By the year 200 B.C. the Buddhist *Tripitaka*, that is, the triple basket, or canon in three parts, was practically complete.

The Tripitaka

1. *The Vinaya Pitaka:* the Discipline Basket, the rules of the monastic life:
   (a) *Sutta Vibhanga*
   (b) *Khandhakas*
      (1) Mahavagga.
      (2) Chullavagga.
   (c) *Parivara.*

(This part of the Buddhist canon was kept secret by the monks, and was not revealed even to the Buddhist laity. Most of the monastic orders seem to have refused to divulge their disciplinary rules.)

2. *The Sutta Pitaka:* the Sermon Basket, the teaching of the Buddha:
   (a) *Digha Nikaya*
   (b) *Majjhima Nikaya*
   (c) *Samyutta Nikaya*
   (d) *Anguttara Nikaya*
   (e) *Khuddaka Nikaya*
3. *The Abhidhamma Pitaka:* the Exposition Basket, an enlarged and detailed treatment of Buddhist doctrine:
   (a) *Dhamma Sangani*
   (b) *Vibhanga*
   (c) *Katha Vatthu*
   (d) *Puggala Pannatti*

(e) *Dhatu Katha*

(f) *Yamakas*

(g) *Patthana*

Many of these *suttas* are beautiful as literature, and are filled with a love of righteousness and a mounting passion for spiritual things which give them great distinction.

Buddhist Teaching in Verse

Do not follow the evil law! Do not live on in thought-lessness! Do not follow false doctrine! Be not a friend of the world.

Rouse thyself! Do not be idle! Follow the law of virtue! The virtuous rests in bliss in this world and in the next.

Follow the law of virtue; do not follow that of sin. The virtuous rests in bliss in this world arrd in the next.

Look upon the world as you would on a bubble, look upon it as you would on a mirage; the king of death does not see him who thus looks down upon the world.

Come, look at this world, glittering like a royal chariot; the foolish are immersed in it, but the wise do not touch it.

He who formerly was reckless and afterwards became sober, brightens up this world, like the moon when freed from clouds.

He whose evil deeds are covered by good deeds, brightens up this world, like the moon when freed from clouds.

This world is dark, few only can see here; a few only go to heaven, like birds escaped from the net.

The uncharitable do not go to the world of the gods; fools only do not praise liberality; a wise man rejoices in liberality, and through it becomes blessed in the other world.

Better than sovereignty over the earth, better than going to heaven, better than lordship over all worlds, is the reward of Sotapatti; the first step in holiness.

—*Dhammapada*

When Buddhism was destroyed in India, this literature perished also, but it has been most faithfully preserved in Ceylon. The language of the *Tripitaka* is called *Pali*. This is not the name of any old Indian vernacular, but merely the Singhalese word for 'text' which has come to be used to designate the language of the text, in contrast with the Singhalese of the commentary. Scholars have not been able to decide as yet which of the old Indian vernaculars, through being used by the monks who won Srilanka to the faith, has been preserved for us in the Pali text.

Jain teaching was similarly handed down, but reached its permanent form later still.

Many other schools had their traditional *suktas*, but they were necessarily lost when the school died out.

The Incarnation Period

परित्राणाय साधूनां विनाशाय च दुष्कृताम्।
धर्मसंस्थापनार्थाय संभवामि युगे युगे।।

To save the righteous, to deslroy evil-doers, to establish the Law,
I come into birth age after age.

—*Bhagavadgita*, iv. 8,

History. The largest fact in the history of these centuries is the irruption of hordes of invaders from Central Asia across the Indus both in the north and in the south. Necessarily these invasions created great disturbances, and produced considerable mixture in the population of the frontier provinces. The break-up of the Asokan Empire also led to many revolutions and upheavals. There was thus much violence and frequent political change throughout these centuries in Northern and Central India. We need not here catalogue the many various dynasties which followed each other east, west, north, and south. We need only notice the rise of the one great empire which appeared during our period.

This was the kingdom of the Kushans, a people from central Asia, their greatest ruler being Kanishka. Peshawar was their capital; and that city, during the first and second centuries of our era, was the centre of a flourishing civilisation in which Indian ideas mingled freely with the influence of Persia and of the Roman Empire. These kings would appear to have favoured Hinduism and Zoroastrianism quite as much as Buddhism; yet the latter religion clearly dominated the country round Peshawar.

Architecture flourished, and a famous school of sculpture arose under Greek influence. The art of the kingdom is known as Gandharan art. Buddhism found a new base for its operations in Peshawar; and Sanskrit first came to the front as the common language of India in the Kushan Empire.

Religion. Under Asoka and his obscure successors Buddhism was greatly favoured. Vast sums of money were spent on Buddhist buildings; and it seems dear from Asoka's edicts that various laws and regulations were enforced which would please Buddhist monks and would displease Brahmins. With the fall of the great empire and the rise of the Sungas to power in Magadha, the tables were turned; for the new dynasty favoured the Brahmins as much as the old favoured Buddhism. Patanjali, founder of the Yoga philosophy, was the priest of Pushyamitra, the first Sunga king, and refers to his celebration of the Asvamedha, or houre-sacrifice, which is a public claim to imperial power. The influence and favour of the court led to great literary activity on the part of the priests.

The main feature of the religious history of the period as a whole is this, that Hinduism and Buddhism now stand opposed to each other as rivals, yet influence each other very greatly in many ways.

RELIC-CASKET

Discovered in the ruins of Kanishka's stupa at Peshawar. The casket is of dark metal and is seven inches high. Contained a rock-crystal reliquary containing bones, said to be Buddha's. On top of casket Buddha and two other figures. Note the haloes. Beneath is Kanishka himself.

Incarnation

One very noteworthy change occurred in Hinduism at this time and, as we shall see, a similar change passed over Buddhism. While at the beginning of the fifth century B.C. Rama and Krishna were but human heroes, they were already worshipped in the time of Megasthenes, the Seleucid ambassador at the court of Chandragupta; and by the opening of the second century B.C. they were acknowledged to be incarnations of Vishnu. In the first and last books of tbe *Ramayana,* which were written in the second century B.C., Rama is represented as an incarnation of half the essence of Vishnu, and in the additions made to the *Mahabharata* about the same time, Krishna is regarded as a miror divinity and in some sense as an incarnation of Vishnu.

During the next three centuries **this rich warm worship of incarnate divinities became entwined with the philosophy of the Atman, and first Krishna and then Rama rose to the lofty position of incarnations of the Supreme.** Krishna occurs in this guise in the latest parts of the *Mahabharata,* dating perhaps from the second century A.D., and also in the *Bhagavadgita.*

Hindu Incarnation

Krishna speaks at the battle of Kurukshetra—

'Many births of Me and thee have passed, O Arjuna. I know them all; but thou knowest them not, O affrighter of the foe.

Though birthless and unchanging of essence, and though lord of born beings, yet in My sway over the Nature that is Mine own I come into birth by My own Magic.

For whensoever the Law fails and lawlessness uprises, O thou of Bharata's race, then do I bring Myself to bodied birth.

THE BOAR INCARNATION OF VISHNU

This relief is at Mahavellipore. It represents Vishnu in his boar avatara with his wife Lakshmi. Beneath is a five-hooded Naga, or divine snake.

To guard the righteous, to destroy evil-doers, to establish the Law, I come into birth age after age.

He who knows in verity My divine birth and works comes not again to birth when he has left the body, he comes to Me, O Arjuna.

The Four Castes were created by Me according to the orders of Moods and Works; know that I am indeed the doer of that work, yet no worker, unchanging.

Father of this universe am I, mother, ordainer, grandsire, the thing that is known and the being that makes clean, the word *Om*, the Rik, the Sama, and the Yajus;

The way, the supporter, the lord, the witness, the dwelling, the refuge, the friend, the origin, the dissolution, the abiding-place, the house of ward, the changeless seed.'

—*Bhagavadgita, iv*

Vishnuism

Certain of the old myths of the Vedas and Brahmanas were transformed into incarnations of Vishnu, and others were created. The series of semi-animal and other incarnations *(avataras*) which are supposed to have preceded Rama and Krishna was thus formed. This long line of Vishnuite incarnations is parallel to the long list of mythical Buddhas which grew up in the Buddhist Church and the similar list of mythical Tirthakaras which took form in Jainism at this time. These new forms of faith, so well calculated to stir emotion and to provoke enthusiastic worship, naturally led to a great growth of Vishnuism. The leading school of Vishnuites were called Bhagavatas, i.e., worshippers of the Bhagavan, the Adorable Lord. **Unlike the teachers of the Vedanta, who held that only the three highest castes could reach Release, because they alone were allowed to read the Upanishads, the Bhagavatas offered salvation to all.**

HINDU IDOLATRY

A coin of Kadphises II, the Kushan king who preceded Kanishka. The reverse gives us Siva with his bull and his trident. First century A.D.

The Cult of Siva

But the cult of Siva did not lag behind. The sacred bull became his companion; the trident was connected with him; the phallic symbol, the *linga,* was adopted for his worship; and he was represented as the typical ascetic. Vishnu in his incarnations, and Siva with these fresh attractions, now stand side by side with Brahma. The words *Saivas* and *Vaishnavas* are used for the followers of these gods.

Six Systems of Philosophy

It was during this period that the six systems of philosophy which are recognised as orthodox by Hindus were worked out in detail. Each took shape in its own school, gradually developed and expounded by a succession of teachers. They expressed the system in sutras in the briefest possible way, and explained the sutras by means of a commentary.

1. The *Karma Mimamsa,* 'work inquiry', the philosophy of sacrifice, founded on the Srauta Sutra. Jaimini wrote the main treatise, the *Karma Mimamsa Sutra.*
2. The *Uttara Mimamsa,* 'later inquiry', the philosophy of the Upanishads, the Vedanta, systematised by Badarayana in his work known as the *Vedanta Sutra,* the *Brahma Sutra,* or the *Sariraka Sutra.*
3. The *Sankhya,* a dualistic atheism, ascribed to the early sage Kapila. No early treatise survives.
4. The *Yoga.* In this system the Sankhya metaphysic is combined with a personal God and with bodily and mental exercises called *Yoga.* Patanjali, of the second

BUDDHIST CHAITYA

At Karle, near Pune. In these assembly-halls a small stupa, introduced to inspire meditation, led to worship. Here we have the nave with its apse, and the stupa taking the place of the altar. There are aisles behind the fine pillars. First century B.C.

century B.C., is the author of the manual, which is called the *Yoga Sutra.*

5. The *Vaiseshika.* This system classifies all phenomena under logical categories, and attributes the origin of the world to atoms. The author of the manual, which is known as the *Vaiseshika Sutra,* is remembered by the nickname Kanada, 'atom-eater'.
6. The *Nyaya* accepts the metaphysic of the Vaiseshika, and adds a very detailed and acute exposition of formal logic. The manual, which is by Gautama, is called the *Nyaya Sutra.*

Many of these ancient sutra manuals have perished, but several survive, of which the greatest is the manual of the Vedanta school, the *Vedanta-Sutra* of Badarayana.

From the Vedanta Sutra

A literal translation of each sutra is given in italics, and then the meaning follows in roman.

Then therefore Brahman-inquiry.

Here beginneth the inquiry into Brahman.

Where the birth, etc., of this.

Brahman is that from which the creation, preservation, and destruction of this world proceed.

From being the source of Scripture.

The omniscience of Brahman follows from its being the source of Scripture.

But that from immediate connexion.

But that Brahman is to be known from Scripture, because it is connected with the Upanishads as their purport.

IMAGE OF BUDDHA

Beside the bodhi tree at Anuradhapura, Srilanka.

From seeing not, unscriptural.

On account of seeing (i.e., thinking) being attributed in the Upanishads to the cause of the world, the *pradhana* of the Sankhya philosophy is not to be identified with the cause indicated by the Upanishads; for it is not founded on Scripture.

If figurative, no, from word Self.

If it be said that the word 'seeing' is used figuratively, we deny that, on account of the word Self being applied to the cause of the world.

—Badarayana, *Vedanta Sutra, I*

Buddhism, which originally was an agnostic philosophy attempting to do the work of a religion, early developed the beginnings of a worship, as we have already seen. During the first half of this period another step was taken. **Images of Buddha, his chief disciples, the previous Buddhas and Maitreya, the coming Buddha, were set up at the stupas, in pagodas and chaityas.** Though the original purpose was merely to stimulate meditation, and though the monks usually kept themselves to that, the necessary result was that the common people worshipped the images. Offerings of flowers and fruit were presented to them; incense and tapers were burned before them; and prayers were uttered with humble adoration and fervent praise. Thus far early Buddhism went; and we have this form still preserved for us practically unaltered in Myanmar and Srilanka.

Mahayana

But the kingdom of the Kushans was the scene of a still more significant change. Buddhism up to this time had contained many philosophic schools, but there had been no schism. In the great intellectual activity of the Kushan Empire, however, there came a development of worship

BODHISATTVA FROM YUSUFZAI

and theology which **split the Buddhist world in two.** The new system, which finally received the name **Mahayana (great path)** in contrast with the old, which was called **Hinayana (humble path),** soon became very popular. In it we meet the new doctrine, borrowed from Hinduism, that behind all things there is the universal soul of which the Buddhas are but manifestations.

Under the old system the great ideal for the monk was to become an *arhat,* that is, a perfect man, destined at death to pass into *nirvana;* but **the ideal of the Mahayana was the Bodhisattva, a being who might become a Buddha and enter nirvana but denies himself that luxury,** so that he may remain in the heavenly regions a gracious and powerful divinity ready to help those that appeal to him. But the chief difference lies in this, that the Hinayana saved the few, while the Mahayana offered Release to the many.

The leaders of the Mahayana treated the Buddhas and the Bodhisattvas as gods, and set up a most elaborate system of worship. In front of the images in the chaitya an altar was erected on which offerings were made. The chaitya thus became a temple and the monk a priest divinity. Each accessory that was likely to make the worship attractive and pleasing to the people was added—richly decorated altars, paintings, gorgeous robes, music, processions, banners, incense, etc. Thus Buddhism, originally an agnostic philosophy, became one of the polytheisms and idolatries of the world. The list of the Budhhas is given later.

Buddha himself was transformed into a Saviour god, incarnate for the good of men, as we may see from the *Lalita Vistara,* the *Saddharma Pundarika,* and other works of the first and second centuries A.D. Thus the same spirit that worked in Hinduism now worked in Buddhism. The *Gita* and the *Saddharma Pundarika* are parallel compositions.

MAHAYANA WORSHIP

Small stupa with image of Buddha carved on it, at Kanheri, near Mumbai.

BUDDHIST INCARNATION

Gautama the Buddha speaks on Gridhrakuta—

'An inconceivable number of thousands of kotis of Aeons, never to be measured, is it since I reached superior enlightenment and never ceased to teach the law.

I roused many Bodhisattvas and established them in Buddha-knowledge. I brought myriads of kotis of beings, endless, to full ripeness in many kotis of Aeons.

I show the place of extinction, I reveal to all beings a device to educate them, albeit I do not become extinct at the time, and in this very place continue preaching the law.

Repeatedly am I born in the world of the living.

What reason should I have to continually manifest mystelf? When men become unbelieving, unwise, ignorant, careless, fond of sensual pleasures, and from thoughtless-ness run into misfortune.

Then I, who know the course of the world, declare, "I am the Tathagata," and consider, How can I incline them to enlightenment? How can they become partakers of the Buddha-laws?

So am I the Father of the world, the Self-born, the Healer, the Protector of all creatures. Knowing them to be perverted, infatuated, and ignorant, I teach final rest, myself not being at rest.

—Saddharma Pundarika, xv.

Amitabha

The, most interesting of all the new divinities of this date is Amitabha, who is described in the *Amitayus Sutra* and a number of other books written in North India during this period. This Buddha is said to live now in a glorious paradise in the West; but, when he was still a Bodhisattva,

Mahayana Worship

A piece of devotional sculpture from the Kushan Empire, found at Sahri Bahlol in Pakistan. Gautama Buddha is in the centre, Avalokitesvara on the left, Maitreya on the right. These two are Bodhisattvas.

he vowed that he would never accept *nirvana* until some means were provided whereby all mankind would be able to receive salvation through faith in him. The worship of this imaginary god cannot now be traced in the history of ancient India, except in sculpture; but it was carried into China, where he is still worshipped, and into Japan, where the two most vigorous sects of the present times are worshippers of Amida, the Japanese corruption of Amitabha.

Literalure. During the first half of this period the scholars of India began to use the art of writing for their books. The Buddhist *Tripitaka* was reduced to writing in Srilanka about 85 B.C., and we may be certam that about the same time or earlier, a similar process was carried out in India among Hindus as well as Buddhists.

Dharmasutra

We found in each Brahmanical school the subject of *dharma,* or the right behaviour of the Hindu in every station of life, dealt with in a Dharmasutra. In this new period these rules of conduct were gradually rewritten in a popular versified form to be used by the Hindu householder outside the schools. The poems thus produced are known as the Dharmasastras. The greatest of all these law-books is the *Manava Dharamsutra.* Its growth seems to cover several centuries. It had reached its present shape by A.D. 200. One of the momentous changes in Hindu life which this fresh code enables us to realise is this, that all widows, even virgin child-widows, were by this time forbidden to remarry.

Excommunication

This passage sets forth so clearly a number of the elements of the Hindu system. Here we have the sanctity of the Veda, the

MAHAYANA WORSHIP

A bronze image of Vairochana, a Buddha of light, at Nara, in Japan. It is 53½ feet in height.

privileges of Brahmins, the restrictions of caste, the sacred cord, the lock of hair on the crown of the head, and excommunication carried out by the performance of the funeral ceremony and *interdictio aqua,* an old Aryan custom. The law here stated as applicable to a Brahmin father who has to be excommunicated by his own son is of course all the more applicable to caste-breakers of lower degree.

Let him cast off a father who assassinates a king, who sacrifices for Sudras, who sacrifices for his own sake, accepting money from Sudras, who divulges the Veda to persons not authorised to study it, who kills a learned Brahmin, who dwells with men of the lowest castes, or cohabits with a female of one of the lowest castes. Having assembled the sinner's spiritual Gurus and the relatives by marriage, the sons and other kinsmen shall perform for him all the funeral rites, the first of which is the libation of water, and afterwards they shall overturn his water-vessel in the following manner; a slave or a hired servant shall fetch an impure vessel from a dust-heap, fill it with water taken from the pot of a female slave and, his face turned towards the south, upset it with his foot, pronouncing the sinner's name and saying: 'I deprive N.N. of water.' All the kinsmen shall touch the slave, passing their sacrificial cords over the right shoulder and under the left arm, and untying the locks on their heads. The spiritual Gurus and the relatives by marriage shall look on.

—Gautama, *Dharmasutra,* xx. 1-6.

Ramayana

It seems most likely that the first and the last books of the *Ramayana* were added about the beginning of our period. Here Rama is represented as an incarnation of half the essence of Vishnu and the *Ramayana* thereby becomes; a Vishnuite work. About the same time large additions were made to the *Mahabharata,* which made it an epic of 24,000 slokas. In the new text Krishna is a demi-god. The recreation and re-publication of these great works, which glorify Hindu kings and Hindu life and worship, was almost certainly carried out under the patronage of the Sungas.

About four centuries later (A.D. 200) vast quantities of new text were introduced into the *Mahabharata,* transforming the epic into a didactic library. Among the additions was the *Bhagavadgita.* Here and elsewhere in the new matter Krishna is represented as the Atman incarnate.

The two epics are the earliest popular literature of India. They sprang from the heart of the people; and though the *Ramayana* was edited for a sectarian purpose, and the *Mahabharata* has been changed by the Brahmins into an immeasurable mass of priestly laws and traditions, they are still greatly beloved hy the people; and, unlike the Vedic literature, they may be read by women, and by men of any caste.

Bhagavadgita

The *Bhagavadgita* or "Song of the Adorable" which is largely a product of Bhagavata theology, is one of the most noteworthy pieces of literature produced in India. **It is the noblest and purest expression of modern Hinduism.** The author wished to produce a poem to express his own boundless reverence for Krishna, to gather the best thoughts of the Upanishads and unite them with the most helpful parts of the philosophies, and at the same time to bind people to the ordinary life and worship of Hindu society. His book was not intended to be a class-book to be used in a Vedic school or by a few hermits in a forest, but a manual which the farmer, the soldier, the shopkeeper, and the Brahmin might read day by day, while pursuing their ordinary avocations.

He did not wish to turn men into sannyasis, but wished to present a religious system which people might accept and use, while they continued their ordinary daily work and lived within the caste system. The two most significant points in his teaching are the supremacy of Krishna and the theory of Karma-yoga. The significance of Krishna lies in this, that he is conceived as the absolute Brahman, the object of all the meditation of the sages of the Upanishads, and at the same time as a personal god approachable with sacrifice and prayer, like other personal gods. The significance of Karma-yoga also lies in its combination of philosophy with the popular life: as Krishna unites the loftiest meditation of the philosopher with the simplest worship of the ignorant, so Karma-yoga unites philosophic renunciation of the world with practical everyday life.

The commands of Karma-yoga are: Give up all desire or the fruits of action, and thereby fulfil the philosophic ideal, but continue to do your ordinary work in the world at the same time, and thus fulfil your duty as a member of a Hindu family and caste. The author of the *Gita* is as anxious to persuade his readers to fulfil all the rules of caste laid down in the *Dharmasastras,* as he is to make them rise to the philosophic contemplation of the absolute Brahman. No other Hindu book has laid hold of the educated classes with the same power as the *Gita.*

Buddhas, Avataras and Tirthakaras

Buddhas	*Avataras of Vishnu*		*Trithakaras*
Mythical—			
Dipamkara			
Kondanna			Rishabhadeva
Mangala	*Matsya[1]:	the Fish	Ajitanatha
Sumanas	*Kurma:	the Tortoise	Sambhavanatha
Revata	*Varaha:	the Boar	Abhinandana
Sobhita	*Narasimha:	the Man-lion	Sumatinatha
Anomadassin	*Vamana:	the Dwarf	Padmaprabha
Paduma	*Parasu-Rama		Suparsvanatha
Narada	*Rama		Chandraprabha
Padumuttara	*Krishna		Suvidhinatha

Sumedha	Vyasa	Sitalanatha
Sujata	Prithu	Sreyamsanatha
Piyadassin	Hari	Vasupujya
Atthadassin	Hamsa	Vimalanatha
Dhammadassin	Manvantara	Anantanatha
Siddhattha	Yajna	Dharmanatha
Tissa	Rishabha	Sautinatha
Pussa	Hayagriva	Kunthunatha
Vipassin	Dhruva	Aranatha
Sikhin	Dhanvantari	Mallinatha
Vessabhu	Nara and Narayana	Munisuvrata
Kakusandha	Dattatreya	Naminatha
Konagamana	Kapila	Neminatha
Kassapa	Sanaka	Parsvanatha
Historical—		
Gautama	*Buddha[2]	Mahavira
Future—		
Maitreya	*Kalki	

1. The ten *avataras* of Vishnu which are usullly met with are marked with asterisks.
2. The Buddha *avatara* of Vishnu is really Gautama, the historical Buddha. One of the many means employed by Hindus to overcome Buddhism was to recognize the Buddha as a Hindu incarnation.

Mahayana Books

About the Christian era the great book of Mahayana Buddhism began to be written. Some of the early ones are in the vernaculars, but very soon Sanskrit comes to the front, and thereafter every great Buddhist work was written in Sanskrit. A very large literature sprang up in North India at this time. Many most famous and influential works might be mentioned, the *Questions of King Milinda,* the *Lalita Vistara,* the *Saddharma Pundarika,* the *Buddhacharita,* the *Amitayus Sutra,* etc. These and many of the books of the old Tripitaka were carried over to China and translated into Chinese by competent scholars, both Indian and Chinese.

Mahayanists formed a canon for themselves, consisting mainly of new Mahayana texts but also including large parts of the old canon. In arrangement it is a Tripitaka also. This canon has been lost in India, but is preserved in distinct forms in Tibet and in China. The student will most readily get some idea of it by looking through Bunyiu Nanjio's *Catalogue of the Chinese Translation of the Buddhist Tipitaka.*

Chronology of the Incarnation Period

External	*History and Religion*	*Literature*		
184 B. C.	184 B.C. Fall of Asokan Empire	Second Stage of *Mahabharata*		Books I and VII of *Ramayana*
100 B.C.	Images in Buddhism			
	72 Fall of Sunga Dynasty			
44 Caesar murdered				
31 Augustus supreme				
29 Christ crucified	Gondophares		Mahayana Leaders	
The New Testa-ment	Kanishka		Asvaghosha	Gradual Trans-lation of Buddhist Books into Chinese
AD. 100		Third Stage of *Mahabharata*	Nagarjuna	
A.D. 200	Krishna as the Atman	*The Gita*		
Christianity in Malabar		*Manava Dharama-sastra*	Aryadeva	
A.D. 300 Constantine grants Christians toleration, A. D. 320				

THE PURANAS

नमस्तुङ्गशिरश्चुम्बिचन्द्रचामरचारव।
त्रैलोक्यनगरारम्भमूलस्तम्भाय शंभवे।।

'Adoration to Sambhu, adorned with the chowrie-like moon on his lofty brow, main pillar in the building of the city of the three worlds!'

—*Harshacharita*, Bana

History. Our period opens with the rise of the great dynasty of the Guptas, who reigned at Patna, but later moved up to Ayodhya. Under their empire North India enjoyed a period of really good government, worthy of comparison with the time of Asoka. The two greatest kings of the dynasty were Samudragupta and Chandragupta II Vikramaditya. The latter king conquered Malwa and probably lived from time to time in Ujjain; so that he may be the reality behind all the mythical tales told about the great Vikramaditya of Ujjain.

This dynasty went down before the attacks of the Shakas, and Huns. **These invaders behaved with monstrous cruelty and violence during the fifty years they were in India. They destroyed Patna. They sacked Buddhist monasteries, massacred the monks, and even killed the Patriarch.** They were driven out, however, in A.D. 528; and from that time onward until the invasions of Mahmud of Ghazni about A.D. 1000, India was comparatively free from foreign attack.

About A.D. 550 a powerful dynasty known as the Chalukyas arose at Badami in Dharwar and played a great part in South Indian politics and civilization for two centuries; while on the other coast at Kanchi the Pallavas ruled the surrounding country.

During the seventh century another brilliant figure appears in North India, the famous Harsha of Kanauj. He spent many years in conquest, and finally was the acknowledged sovereign of the whole of North India from the Himalayas to the Narbada. He was fortunate in having at his court a distinguished literary figure named Bana, who wrote an historical romance setting forth the great deeds of his patron. We also hear a good deal about the Chinese traveller Huen Tsang, who was greatly honoured by him. Our period closes with his empire.

Religion. Hinduism during this period is chiefly marked by a popular sectarianism. The follower of Siva or of Vishnu uses the most extravagant language in praising his own God and curses the devotees of the other heartily. An attempt was made to reconcile all sectaries by the doctrine of the three-fold manifestation of the Supreme in Brahma, Vishnu, and Siva; but the concept never truly laid hold of the Hindu people. The Triad is frequently mentioned, and it is now and then represented in sculpture; but it was Siva and Vishnu that drew the reverence of men. The mythology of the time is extravagant

Vishnu as Saviour of the Gods

An Example of Puranic Mythology

The gods addressed the mighty Vishnu thus—
'Conquered in battle by the evil demons,
We fly to thee for succour, Soul of all:
Pity and by thy might deliver us.'
Hari the lord, creator of the world,
Thus by the gods implored, all graciously
Replied—'Your strength shall be restored, ye gods;
Only accomplish what I now command;
Unite yourselves in peaceful combination
With these your foes; collect all plants and herbs
Of diverse kinds from every quarter; cast them
Into the sea of milk; take Mandara,
The mountain, for a churning-stick, and Vasuki,

THE MARRIAGE OF SIVA AND PARVATI

The serpent, for a rope; together churn
The ocean to produce the beverage—
Source of all strength and immortality;
Then reckon on my aid. I will take care
Your foes shall share your toil, but not partake
In its reward or drink th' immortal draught;'
Thus by the god of gods advised, the host
United in alliance with the demons.
Straightway they gathered various herbs and cast them
Into the waters, then they took the mountain
To serve as churning-staff, and next the snake
To serve as cord, and in the ocean's midst
Hari himself, present in tortoise-form,
Became a pivot for the churning-staff.

—*Vishnu Purana,* i. 9

In this period the myths about Krishna underwent considerable embellishment. The story of his childhood was told in great detail. His cowherd exploits also took form at this time and captured the masses. All this fresh mythology had its centre in Mathura and Vrindavana. Clearly the cult of Krishna was carried on there with great fervour.

Hinduism and Buddhism drew nearer and nearer to each other during these centuries, each borrowing from the other, both becoming coarser, but Hinduism continuously gaining in popularily. It was a period of decadence; but Hinduism had by far the stronger constitution.

Expansion of Buddhism

This period saw a very great expansion of Buddhism in other lands. It became supreme in China; and throughout the period numerous Indian scholars went to China to teach

BUDDHIST IMAGE

From Java. Note the great halo.

the faith, while many Chinese pilgrims found their way to India. The translation of Buddhist texts into Chinese went on apace, both Indians and Chinese doing large service in this way. From China the religion passed into Korea and Japan. Devoted missionaries carried it to Myanmar, Siam, and Java, and won the populations of those lands. Its influence spread far and wide over the whole of Central and Eastern Asia. India was its home, and there its most famous scholars studied and taught. The greatest university of Buddhism, Nalanda in Bihar, was founded during the sixth century, and was adorned by a long succession of great scholars for at least two centuries thereafter. The philosophy of Buddhism at this time shows a great approximation to Hindu thought.

Literature. The Guptas were great patrons of literature. The earliest existing Puranas, which embody the sectarian religion of the period, seem to date from their time; and every branch of secular literature rose to splendour under their fostering care, the Drama, Kavya poetry, Rhetoric, Grammar, Astronomy, Romance. The word *Purana* means *archaeo-logica,* and was first used of old-world myths and tales about the origin of things.

The existing Puranas, however, are sectarian in Sanskrit verse, written to catch the popular ear and secure worshippers for Vishnu, Siva, or Brahma. Each begins with an account of the origin of the world, but soon becomes a panegyric of the favourite divinity. Men of any caste, and women too, are allowed to read the Puranas.

THE LEADING DIVINITIES OF THE HINDU PANTHEON

The incomprehensible *Brahman* is manifested in the Triad—Brahma, Vishnu, Siva.

ROCK-CUT SHRINE
At Mahavellipore

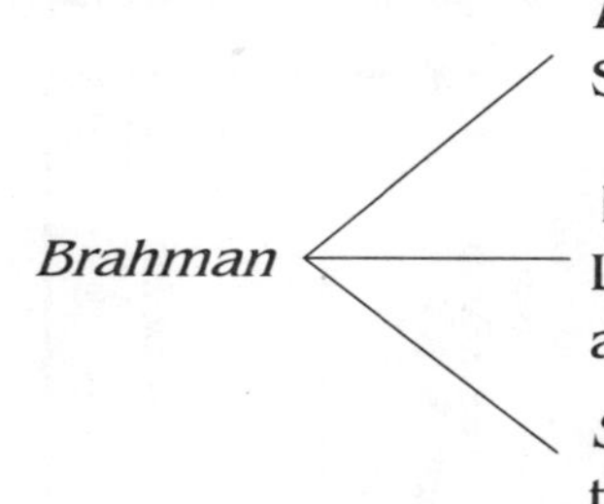

Brahma, the Creator, married Sarasvati, the goddess of learning.

Vishnu, the Preserver, married Lakshmi, the goddess of wealth, also called Sri.

Siva, the Destroyer, married Uma, the daughter of Himalaya. She is also called Parvati, Durga, Kali, Bhavani.

Their sons are *Ganesa,* the elephant-headed god, whose functions are somewhat like those of the Roman Janus, and Kartikeya, called also Subrahmanya, Skanda and Kumara, the god of war.

Buddhist literature at this time consisted mostly of philosophic works produced by the scholars of Nalanda.

The Svetambara Jain canon received its final form in A.D. 454.

Living Souls in Jainism

This extract is inserted here as an example of the characteristic teaching of the Jains. Similar statements follow in the same *Sutra* with reference to living souls in fire, water, and air.

The living world is afflicted, miserable, difficult to instruct, and without discrimination. In this world full of pain, suffering by their different acts, see the benighted ones cause great pain. See! there are beings individually embodied in earth; not one all-soul. See! there are men who control themselves, whilst others only pretend to be houseless, i.e., monks such as the Buddhists, whose conduct differs not from that of householders, because one destroys this earth-body by bad and injurious doings,

TEMPLE OF MUKTESVARA

At Bhubanesvara. A small but beautiful shrine of the Indo-Aryan style. The ornamental arch in front, called a Torana, is very graceful.

and many other beings besides, which he hurts by means of earth, through his doing acts relating to earth.

As somebody may cut or strike a blind man who cannot see the wound; as somebody may cut or strike the foot, the ankle, the knee, the thigh, the hip, the navel, the belly, the flank, the back, the bosom, the heart, the breast, the neck, the arm, the finger, the nail, the eye, the brow, the forehead, the head; as some kill openly; as some extirpate secretly; thus the earth-bodies are cut, struck, and killed, though their feeling is not manifest. He who injures these earth-bodies does not comprehend and renounce the sinful acts; he who does not injure these, comprehends and renounces the sinful acts. Knowing them, a wise man should not act sinfully towards earth, nor cause others to act so, nor allow others to act so. He who knows these causes of sin relating to earth, is called a reward-knowing sage. Thus I sav.

— *Acharanga Sutra*

Great Architecture

During this period architecture was cultivated with zeal and success by Buddhists, Jains, and Hindus. A great deal of the finest cave-work dates from this time. Very few buildings, however, belonging to these centuries remain above ground. Yet one of the most beautiful, the great Buddhist pagoda at Bodh Gaya, has survived, though probably much altered. The rich cluster of Hindu temples at Bhubanesvar in Orissa are also still standing. They are of the Indo-Aryan style.

A Hindu or Jain temple consists of a cubical cell, lighted only from the door, but surmounted by a tower. The image is placed in the cell, which thus becomes the shrine. The tower marks the position of the shrine. Usually a porch stands in front of the door of the shrine.

ROCK-CUT SHRINE

At Mahabalipuram. This and the other shrines, known as the Seven Pagodas, are all Hindu work. But the style of this eumple is taken unchanged from a Buddhist *vihara* or monastery. Then this in turn produced the tower of the Dravidian style.

The three leading styles are distinguished from each other by the form of the tower. The Northern or Indo-Aryan tower has curvilinear sides. The Southern or Dravidian tower is pyramidal and in stories. The Chalukyan tower is usually star-shpaed. The earliest existing examples of Dravidian architecture are the Pallava temples of Kanchi and the rock-cut monuments known as the seven Pagodas at Mahabalipuram near Madras, which date from the seventh century. About the same time the Chalukyan style arose in the West.

Puranic Period

External Events	*History and Religion*	*Literature*	
	A.D. 320 Rise of the Guptas, A.D. 326 Samudragupta, A.D. 375 Chandragupta II	Vayu Purana	
Buddhism enters Korea A.D. 400			
	The Iron Pillar at Delhi	Kalidasa Jain Svetambara canon fixed	BUDDHIST SCHOLARS Buddhaghosha
A.D. 500	The Huns, Fall of the Gupta Empire Pataliputra destroyed	Early Puranas edited	
A.D. 552 Buddhism in Japan	A.D. 528 Defeat of the Huns	HINDU ARCHITECTURE	Asanga Vasubandhu
A.D. 600 Muhammad 570-632 Buddhism in Tibet, Siam, Burma and Java	Harsha reigns A.D. 606-647, Huen Tsang in India A.D. 629-646 Persian cross at Kottayam	Rajputana Badami Conjeeveram Mahavellipore Bhubanesvara	Dignaga Gunaprabha Dharmakirti

Poet-Saints and Commentators

> Manikka Vachakar's great saying about Siva: 'Thou mad'st me thine; didst fiery poison eat, pitying poor souls, that I might thine ambrosia taste—I, meanest one.'
>
> —*Tiruvachakam*

History. There are very few outstanding events in the dead, dull level of these five and a half centuries. Muhammedan aggression was almost entirely confined to Sind and the frontier until the latter part of the twelfth century. Yet great ethnic changes were going on. The foreign races which had entered India in the earlier centuries, and the aboriginal races of Bengal and Bihar which had risen to prominence, were gradually absorbed and assimilated by the Hindu people. Numerous tribes were transformed into castes, and their leaders were supplied with a mythical genealogy. From the midst of this creative chaos arose the Rajputs who dominated the centre and the west for several centuries. They were a chivalrous race, and their kingdoms in Malwa, Delhi, Kanauj, Ajmer, and Gwalior showed activity, military courage and high civilization; but their dissensions made them an easy prey, when the Muhammedan invaders came. In the south a number of kingdoms arose and flourished and fell; and the local fortunes of Jainism, of Buddhism, or of some Hindu sect were frequently intertwined with the political change.

Religion and Literature. The steady rise of Hinduism to supremacy and the corresponding decline of Buddhism are the most prominent features of the religious history of this period.

But when we look more closely, we become aware that a subtle change has passed over Hindu faith and practice. **Modern popular Hinduism has been born. The ancient Vedic sacrifices have fallen almost altogether into**

disuse. It is the worship of the temples and the annual festivals celebrated at home that hold the affections or the people. Where philosophic influence is strong, animal sacrifices are prohibited in the temples; but in many places the practice has come in once more, along with many new divinities, from the aboriginal peoples. Processions and shows and dramatic representations are common. Women are kept in most temples as servants of the god.

Another conception seems to have taken shape in this period, the idea that each goddess is the *sakti* or energy of her husband. The god is conceived as retired, absolute, inconceivable: the goddess is a sort of emanation from him, bringing his power down to man, and is a much more approachable being than her lord.

The two great sects, the Vishnuite and the Sivaite, still continue to hold the supreme place in the religion throughout our period. Their systems of worship are now completely developed. The chief difference between Saiva and Vaishnava worship is this, that **Siva is usually represented by the phallic symbol, the *linga* and the *yoni*, while Vishnu is always represened by an image.** The ritual differs in details, but only in details. Vaishnavas never sacrifice animals, and the same is true of all Saivas in South India. The usual offerings are grain, fruit, flowers, and milk. Both sects give *tirtha* and *prasada* to their worshippers, i.e., a portion of the water and of the food which have been offered to the idol.

Both use sect-marks on the forehead and other parts of the body; but the Vaishnavas, in addition, brand on the body the symbols of Vishnu. Both sects pay worship to their teachers, *gurus,* and lay great stress on their ministrations. Both use a *mantra* or watchword, to which they attribute great supernatural power. Both appeal to men

JAIN SCULPTURE

Worship of the Digambara Jains, at Kalugumalai, Tinnevelly.

of all castes; yet both uphold the laws of caste with great rigidness.

The Saktas

During this period a third sect of great importance arose, chiefly in Bengal; the *Saktas* or worshippers of *Kali,* the wife of Siva, as his *sakti.* They fall into two groups, the right-hand and the left-hand Saktas. Both groups show many signs of aboriginal influence, notably animal sacrifice and magic rites; and the basis of the whole cult in both is phallic; but, while the right-hand group are respectable in their worship, **the left-hand Saktas are most immoral. Their cult is based on the five M's, or elements of worship, the Sanskrit names of which begin with M, flesh, wine, women, fish, and finger-signs.** In other points Saktas are like Sivaites.

These sects naturally required manuals describing their worship and sectarian practices. The earliest of these books, which take the place occupied in Vedic worship by the Srauta-sutras, appeared early in this period. Vaishnava manuals are called *Pancharatra Samhitas,* Saiva manuals *Saiva Agamas,* and Sakta manuals *Tantras.* This literature is in Sanskrit, and most of it is in verse. In many respects these books are like the Puranas.

About the same time Buddhism in Bengal and Bihar yielded to the attractions of *sakti-worship* and magic, and developed Tantric thought and practice. **A university filled with this spirit arose at Vikramasila on the Ganges.** Tibet accepted this form of the faith and still remains true to it.

Alvars

The twelve *Alvars* (often called *Azhvars:* they were wandering teachers and poets of various castes) preached

TEMPLE OF SIVA AT TANJORE

This fine stone edifice is Dravidian in style: It was built by Rajaraja the Great, a Chola king, about A.D. 1000.

in South India a popular Vishnuism, which drew its inspiration from the Puranic stories of Krishna. They offered salvation through Vishnu to men of any caste. They caught the ear of the people with their beautiful Tamil hymns. These were finally gathered in a collection, the name of which is the *Nalayira Prabandham,* but which is often referred to as the Tamil Veda. These popular lyrics are still used in the daily worship of most of the Vishnuite temples of the south.

The Praise of Vishnu in Tamil

Two hymns of the greatest of the Alvars, Nammalvar.

The Love of God and of the World

My Father, Lord of worlds evolved, involved, breathes there the man

That sees thy lotus feet with royal signs adorned, which stride

The triple worlds at once, and seeing will not melt away In bliss ambrosial sweet, his heart immersed in joy supreme,

A sweetness ravishing, a sense sublime? —If so, ah fool! He knows not, what for him is highest good, pure love for Thee!

Ah fool, to lose this wealth, and strain his every nerve to win

With mountain-labour short-lived joy or power o'er mortal things,

Ev'n if he sways the triad spheres, or sleeps in heaven's shade.

A Prayer for Release from Transmigration.

Eternal Lord of angels, who dost deign to veil Thy form

In all Creation's varied state, to save poor souls, Vouchsafe in all Thy grace to stay and hear Thy servants' cry,

LINGA SHRINE

This shrine is whitin the cave temple hollowed out of the solid rock in the island of Elephanta, in Mumbai harbour. The figures are *dvarapalas,* door-wardens, keeping the entrance of Siva's residence.

That we be saved the dire return to former wretchedness,
When we mistook the body for the soul, and sinned all sins,
Which clung to us and fixed us evermore to mortal frames.

Adiyars

Contemporaneously the *Adiyars* did a similar service for the religion of Siva. The three greatest of them were Appar, Nana Sambandhar, and Sundarar. Their Tamil hymns form the *Devaram,* or 'Divine Garland', and have exercised a great influence on Saivism. Like the Vishnuites, they offered salvation to all. In the tenth century a still greater man, known as Manikka Vachakar, consecrated his poetic gifts to Siva. He wrote a collection of exquisite Tamil lyrics which form the *Tiruvachakam,* or Sacred Utterance. Both these collections of hymns are used in the worship of Siva in the temples.

The Praise of Siva in Tamil

An extract from one of the hymns of Appar, one of the Saiva Adiyars.

Ritualism Valueless

From hold of moral blame and sin,
O ye who would be truly free!
Adore the holy feet of Him,
Our Dancing Lord, and think of Him
With love and joy. The Watcher will
With you abiding grant His grace.

What though ye be great doctors wise?
What though ye hear the *sastras* read?
What though the duty ye assume
Of doling out cooked food and gifts?
What though ye know the eight and two?

SIVA THE DANCER, NATARAJA

Siva's activity in the world and in the soul is spoken of as sport, and is symbolized in his dance.

It boots him naught who does not feel
The noble truth that God is love.

What though ye roam through lands and wilds?
What though ye faultless penance make?
What though ye give up eating meat
And heav'nward look? None wins reward
But those that praise the knowing Lord.

What though your views are proper, true?
What though ye fast? Upon a hill
What though ye make a penance great?
What though ye bathe and show you fair?
It boots none aught but those that feel
That all through time the Lord endures.

Bhagavatas

In North India the *Bhagavata Purana* or Purana of the Adorable, a rhapsody on Krishna, and by far the most influential of the Puranas, appeared somewhere about the tenth century. Nimbarka, whose followers worship Radha, Krishna's cowherd mistress, as well as Krishna himself, came a little later. Jayadeva, the author of the *Gita Govinda*, or Cowherd Song, which celebrates Krishna in the richest erotic strain, flourished about A.D. 1100. The *Bhakti-sutra* of Sandilya is a non-sectarian philosophic work, defining the Bhagavata doctrine. All these books are in Sanskrit.

Vira Saivas

At Kalyan in the Maratha country in the twelfth century, Basava, the prime minister of the state, founded the Vira Saiva sect. The movement seems to have been essentially a revolt against Brahmin domination. The ancient worship of Siva is retained, only the *linga* and Siva's bull, Nandi, are very prominent. Members of the sect are distinguished from ordinary Hindus by the wearing of a small *linga* some-

TEMPLE OF JAGANNATH AT PURI, ORISSA

A Vishnuite shrine of Indo-Aryan style. Note that there are three porches, each with a pyramidal roof. The curvilinear tower, marking the situation of the shrine, stands out behind. About A. D. 1100.

where about the person. Hence they are commonly called Lingayats. Their priests are called Jangamas. At first they renounced caste completely; but the old poison has crept in amongst them again. Caste had been denounced earlier by Kapilar and Vemana, the first a Tamil, the second a Telugu poet; but **the Vira Saiva sect seems to have been the earliest organised movement that opposed the ancient basis of Hindu society. Similar attempts followed North India.**

Bhakti is one of the most important elements of the teaching of all these sects. *Bhakti* means 'adoration' directed towards Bhagavan, 'the adorable,' by the Bhakta, 'the adoring devotee.' Bhagavan is used to Vishnu, Krishna, Rama, Siva, or any other god the worshipper adores. All the modern *bhakti* schools of Vishnuism are called by the common name of Bhagavatas, worshippers of Bhagavan. This was the name of a very early Vishnuite school.

Sutras on the Nature of Bhakti

1. Now then there is a wish to know faith (i.e., *bhakti*)

2. In Its highest form it is an affection fixed on God.

3. From the promise of immortality to him who abides in Him.

4. If you say, it is knowledge—no, because the knowledge of one who hates Him is not an abiding in Him.

5. And from its inferiority thereto.

6. It is an affection from its being the opposite of hatred and from the Vedic expression 'taste'.

7. It is not an action: for, like knowledge, it does not depend on effort.

8. Hence indeed is the endlessness of its fruit.

CHALUKYAN TEMPLE

At Somnathpur, in Mysore. The star-shaped tower may be distinctly seen. Part of the porch with its pierced slabs of stone is visible also. The date is about A.D. 1050.

9. And from the use of the word 'resignation' *(prapatti)* in the case of one who has knowledge, as in other cases where 'resignation' is used.

10. This (faith) is the main thing, since the others depend upon it.

22. This (faith) is indeed the highest from the express declaration of its superiority to the performers of sacrificial acts, to those who follow knowledge, and to those who practise concentration.

24. But it is not the same as belief. because it has a wider range.

78. All, down even to the despised castes, are capable of learning it at second-hand, like the great common truths.

83. This (highest faith) is the true identity with the Supreme, since this is recognized as the meaning of the *Gita.*

Acharyas

This is also the period of the great *acharyas* or systematic teachers. Each was a sannyasI, and was either the head of a school or the chief priest of a sect. They distinguished themselves by writing, teaching, preaching, and public disputation. Their writings, which are in Sanskrit, are largely commentaries on the sacred books, both *sruti* and *smriti;* but they did large service also in combating Buddhism and Jainism, and some of them were great organisers as well.

The *Karma Mimamsa* and the *Vedanta* were the supreme schools of the time. The other four philosophies had their followers, but they were of comparatively little account. Every sect seems to have accepted Badarayana's *Vedanta-sutra* as an authoritative work.

IMAGE OF SANKARA IN THE KAMACHIAMMA TEMPLE, KANCHI

Note the single rod and the pose of the great teacher's right hand. The smaller image in front represents Sankara also. It is carried in processions, but the great image is never moved.

The first of these famous acharyas is Kumarila, who represents the *Karma Mimamsa* school. He flourished about A.D. 700, and wrote a commentary on the sutras of Jaimini.

Sankara

A little more than a century later there appeared the great Sankara (A.D. 788 to about 850), the supreme acharya of the Vedanta school. His fame rests on his commentaries on the *Vedanta-sutra,* the *Bhagavadgita,* and the chief Upanishads. He held that the true Vedanta system was *advaita,* i. e., an unqualified monism. **Nothing is real except Brahman. Man's soul is the eternial spirit whole and undivided; and the world is maya, illusion. Hence, forward the central school of the Vedanta is advaita**, strictly monistic. His scholarship and immense capacity secured him great influence; and his system of thought was accepted all over India.

From this time onward the central school of the Vedanta accepts the doctrine of incarnations taught in the Gita.

Thus the ancient philosophy attached to itself a theology with the worship of a personal god and the use of idols. Sankara seems also to have accepted and taught the doctrine of the Hindu triad in the philsophic form, that Brahma, Vishnu, and Siva are the triple manifestation of the impersonal One, but that they are not eternal beings. This is the theology of the Smarta Brahmins of South India. But **he did a very great work also by his preaching in all parts of India, by his opposition to the sects that swarmed in his day, by re-arranging the ascetic orders and by the foundation of a number of monasteries for the encouragement of learning,** formed on the mode of Buddhist monasteries.

But, the theistic sects, although they recognized the *Vedanta-sutra* as an inspired work, found it hard to square

GOPURAMS

Of temple of Siva at Tanjore. A Dravidian temple usually stands in a large courtyard, the entrance to which is under a massive gateway called a Gopuram. Early examples such as these are of stone and are modernate in height.

the monistic metaphysic and impersonal theology of Sankara with their religious beliefs.

Extract from a Sankara Commentary

This passage is given here to show the style of the great commentator, Sankara. It is also of interest as expressing the relation of the famous work, the *Vedanta-sutras,* to the *Vedanta-texts,* as the Upanishads are here called.

Some of those who maintain a Lord to be the cause of the world, think that the existence of a Lord different from mere transmigrating beings can be inferred by means of the argument stated just now without recourse being had to Scripture at all—But, it might be said, you yourself in the Sutra under discussion have merely brought forward the same argument! —By no means, we reply. The Sutras, i.e., literally 'the strings', have merely the purpose of stringing together the flowers of the Vedanta-passages. In reality the Vedanta-passages referred to by the Sutras are discussed here. For the comprehension of Brahman is effected by the ascertainment, consequent on discussion, of the sense of the Vedanta-texts, not either by inference or by the other means of right knowledge. While, however, the Vedanta-passages primarily declare the cause of the origin, etc., of the world, inference also, being an instrument of right knowledge in so far as it does not contradict the Vedanta-texts, is not to be excluded as a means of confirming the meaning ascertained. Scripture itself, moreover, allows argumentation; for the passages, *Brihadaranyaka Upanishad,* II. iv. 5, and *Chhandogya Upanishad,* VI. xiv. 2, declare that human understanding assists Scripture.

—Sankara's *Bhashya* to the *Vedanta-Sutras* I. i.

Ramanuja

It was nearly three centuries later before the worshippers of Vishnu produced a man fit to wrestle with Sankara over

BRONZE IMAGE OF RAMANUJA AT SRIPERUBUDUR

This image is said to have been consecrated during Ramanuja's lifetime in the temple of his native place, and may therefore be a portrait. Note the sect-mark on the forehead, the triple rod and the symbol in front, which represents Sathakopa, the great Alvar.

this great question. Their protagonist is Ramanuja, whose mean date is A.D. 1100. He carried on the work of the Alvars, and was high-priest of the whole Vaishnava community of the south. His commentary on the *Vedanta-sutra* is known as the *Sri-bhashya,* and has achieved a popularity almost as great as the work of Sankara. **He calls his system Visishtadvaita, modified monism, and claims that it is the true Vedanta,** the doctrine of the Upanishads. Brahman is Vishnu and is personal. Man's spirit is an *amsa* or portion of God, and even in final union retains its own individuality and consciousness. The doctrine of incarnations is strongly held.

On one point he held a very ambiguous position. As a Vedantist he could speak only to twice-born men; for they only had the right to read the Upanishads. Further, his system was a burdensome one in its rules about eating, bathing, and dressing. But, on the other hand, as the heir of the Alvars, who had preached to all classes of men, he taught the common people Vaishnavism, and even admitted the outcastes on occasion to certain temples.

A century later his followers fell into two sects, the northern school, *Vada-galai,* and the southern school, *Ten-galai.* The chief difference between them lies in the doctrine of the influence of divine grace on the soul, the northern school teaching that it is 'Co-operative', the southern that it is 'Irresistible'. Both hold the doctrine of *bhakti,* 'love, faith, adoration,' and also the doctrine of *prapatti,* 'surrender,' but the southern section make this latter a passive, involuntary resignation correspondent to the irresistible grace of God.

Hence **the former is called the Monkey school, because the young monkey clings to his mother, while**

the latter is the Cat school, because the kitten is carried by the mother.

THE VAISHNAVAS OF THE SOUTH

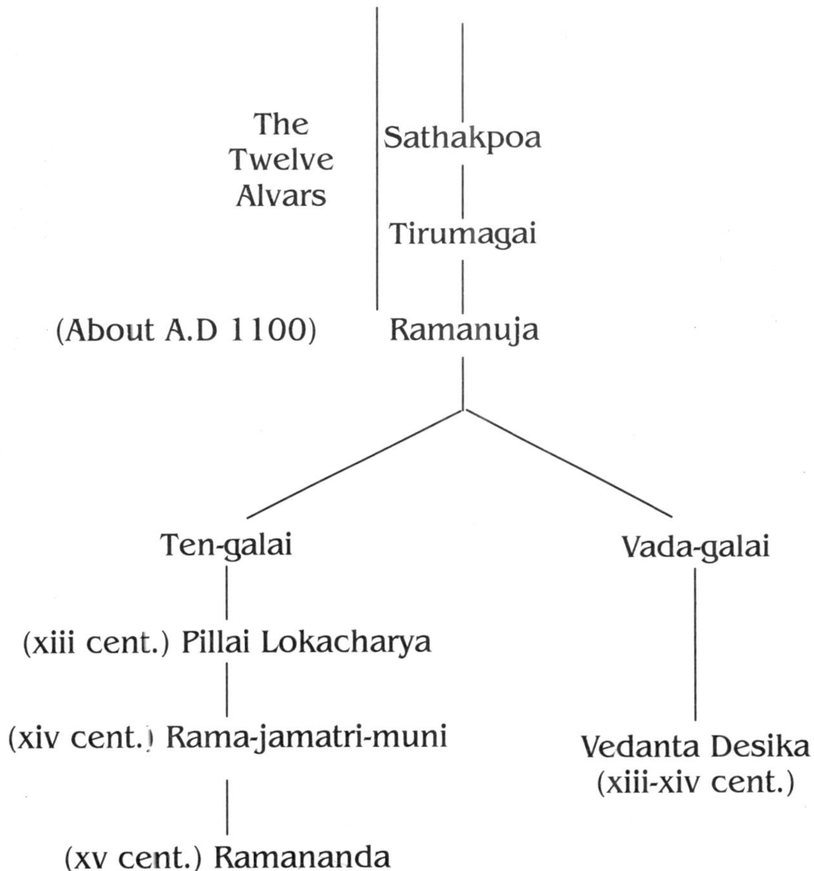

Nilakantha

The acharya of the worshippers of Siva is Nilakantha. In his commentary on the *Vedanta-sutra,* he claims that Brahman is Siva and is personal, and that the soul is distinct from God. Yet the system is called *advaita,* i.e., monistic, the monism being explained in the sense that the individual, though distinct, is inseparable from God, and that when at last the man, achieving Release, approaches God, 'he wears away atom by atom, so that at the moment of union nothing of him is left, and what is left is the Presence of the Supreme one only and the feeling of His Presence, and no feeling, or consciousness of feeling, of himself or others.' The whole doctrine of incarnations is denied, but instead of it there is the doctrine that Siva manifests himself in various forms to his worshippers.

Canon of The Vedanta, the Prasthanatraya

A. THE UPANISHADS. The following eleven are usually studied: *Chhandogya, Kena, Aitareya, Kaushitaki, Isa, Kathaka, Mundaka, Taittiriya, Brihadaranyaka, Svetasvatara, Prasna.*

B. THE BHAGAVADGITA.

C. THE VEDANTA-SUTRA.

In studying these sacred books the *Advaiti* follows Sankara, the *Visishtadvaiti* follows Ramanuja, the *Dvaiti* follows Madhva, and the Saivite sects follow Nilakantha.

It is noticeable that these philosophic leaders, though they were sannyasis and Vedantists, yet lived in the closest co-operation with the temple-worship of the time. They worshipped images, and are themselves represented by images and worshipped to-day in numerous temples throughout India.

During these centuries all the great centres of population were adorned with splendid temples covered with, the most delicate and elaborate sculpture, though here and there horribly defiled by indecency.

CHRONOLOGY OF THE PERIOD

External Events	*History*	*Religion*	*Literature*
A.D. 700			
711 Muham-medans in Sind			Kumarila
732 Europe saved from Islam	The Parsis arrive in India	Rock-cut Temple of Kailas at Ellora	
A. D 800			
		Scond Persian cross at Kottayam Decline of Buddhism	Sankara
A.D. 900			
		Rise of Jainism in the South	*Bhagavata Purana*
A.D. 1000			Manikka Vachakar
	Rajaraja the Great	The great Temple of Tanjore	Nimbarka
1096 The Crusades	A.D.1025 Tempie of Somnath destroyed		
A.D. 1100			
	Conquest of North India by Muham-medans	A.D. 1193 Buddhism crushed in Bengal and Bihar	Ramanuja, *Gita Govinda, Bhakti Sutra*
A. D. 1200			

The Bhakti Period

'The beads are of wood, the gods of stone; the Ganges and the Jumna are water; Rama and Krishna are dead; the Vedas are fictitious stories.'

—*Kabir*

History. The Muhammedan conquest of North India at the very beginning of this period, with the piecemeal conquest of Southern India during the following centuries, is practically all that the history of this period contains. **The violence, bloodshed, and cruelty of the early conquests were followed by the marvellous wisdom, temperance, and justice of Akbar; but his great-grandson Aurangzeb brought back the persecuting horrors and cruelties of the earlier time.** The Hindu kingdom of Vijayanagar withstood for a couple of centuries the whole force of the Muhammadens of the Deccan, but it was overthrown in 1565, in the fierce battle of Talikot. From this time Muhammedan influence had a wider range in South India. From the sixteenth century onward, the Portuguese, the Dutch, the French, and the English were to be found at many points on the seaboard of India; but not until some decades after the battle of Plassey did Europe exercise any serious influence on the life of the people.

Religion and Literature. The Muhammedan conquest of India must not be regarded as merely a series of military exploits leading to a vast political change. The conquerors regarded themselves as crusaders, attacking a vast idolatrous paganism in the name of God. Hence, **wherever they went, they destroyed the religious schools, overthrew the temples, smashed the idols, drove away or killed the Buddhist monks and the Hindu priests.** Idolatry was forbidden, and a tax was Imposed on non-Muslims. It **was their missionary method,** their way of

HINDU PILLARS IN MOSQUE

Beside Qutb Minar, Delhi. This mosque was built from the spoils of twenty seven Hindu and jain temples.

overcoming Hinduism. Muslim policy allowed but little relief or peace tor the Hindu, or opportunity to rebuild, until Akbar arose. Throughout the whole vast territory **In North India where their armies came and went, there is scarcely a fragment of ancient Hindu work left, except what they built into their mosques.**

Buddhism seems to have disappeared almost altogether under the shock; and Hinduism suffered most severely also; for many Hindus became Muslims, and, with the fall of the Hindu kingdoms and the forfeiture of temple lands, school, monastery, and priest were left without income. Hence Sanskrit scholarship and Hindu learning made comparatively little show in North India for a very long time; but at **Vijayanagar a great deal of good work was done. The commentaries of the brothers Sayana and Madhava are of great value.**

Yet Hinduism was too deeply rooted in the hearts of the people to be destroyed by adversity. Though changes necessarily arose as a result of the conquest, it is surprising how little alteration was produced in the religion. Indeed it would not be too much to say that the crushing of the Hinduism of the temple and the scholar led to the outbursting of a simpler and more helpful faith from the heart of the people itself.

The Muslims were later on penetrating into the south. So there we find good architecture still being built, e.g., the temple of Subrahmanya at Tanjore, one of the finest examples of the Dravidian style in existence. **In the sixteenth and seventeenth centuries the greater temples were enclosed with enormous walls and were frequently used as forts.** The gopurams of this period are of enormous height, but their sculpture is of stucco, and the style is everywhere flamboyant and decadent.

QUTB MINAR AT DELHI

The iron pillar dates from Chandragupta II, about A. D. 415. The pillars of the mosque are Hindu and Jain. The Minar, a memorial of the Muslim conquest, dates from about A. D. 1230.

The religious movement of the north during these centuries fall into three groups, Ramaite, Krishnaite, and deistic; yet all the sects have a great many points in common, inherited from earlier forms of Vaishnavism. They believe in one parsonal God who is full of love and pity for those who worship Him; yet all, except the followers of Kabir, recognise the other gods, and worship idols; they all hold that the human soul is a portion of the Divine, and that it will eternally retain its individuality; they offer salvation to men of all castes, demanding faith and *bhakti* toward the Lord; they use the vernaculars instead of Sanskrit; they exalt the *guru,* the religious teacher, to a place of great authority; they use a *mantra,* i.e., a secret phrase or password, which is whispered by the guru to the novice on initiation; they partake of a sacramental meal; and each sect has its own order of ascetics as well as its congregation of the laity.

Ramananda

Of the Ramaite leaders we shall mention the three most notable. Ramananda was a native of South India and was a leader in the Srisampradaya, the church of Ramanuja; but in consequence of a quarrel he left the sect and migrated to North India. He gave up all the exclusiveness of Ramanuja, and also his troublesome restrictions ahout food. He preached in Hindi, and admitted all castes, even the lowest, to his fold. **He had twelve aposties, among whom were a Rajput,** a **currier, a barber, and a Muhammedan weaver.** The whole *bhakti* movement in the north owes a great debt to Ramananda. He belongs to the first half of the fifteenth century; yet his theology and practice show no trace of Muhammedan influence.

SUBRAHMANYA TEMPLE AT TANJORE

The Followers of Ramananda

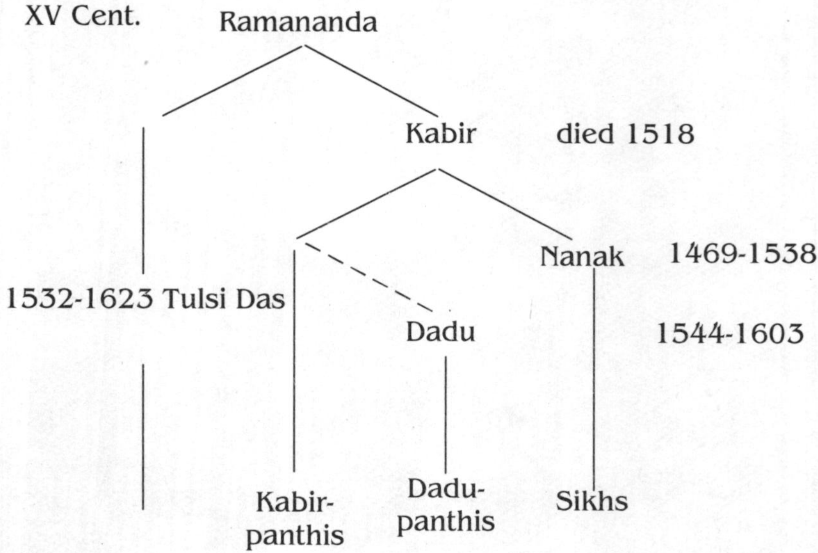

Tulsi Das

Tulsi Das belonged to the church of Ramananda. His activity was contemporaneous with the reign of the great Akbar and of his son Jahangir. He alone among the *bhakti* leaders did not found a sect. He preferred to influence all his fellow - countrymen; and he has won his reward; for the millions of the people of Upper India to-day acknowledge Tulsi Das as their guide.

The teaching which he imparted as he wandered over the land he gave permanent form to in the *Ramacharit Manas,* 'the Lake of the Deeds of Rama'. It is a modern Ramayana in the sense that it recounts the old story, but it is shot through and through with *bhakti* theology and with the healthy moral spirit of the poet. The language is Eastern Hindi. Those who know say that he produced 'some of the most beautiful poetry which has found birth in Asia'; and

GOPURAM AT KUMBAKONAM

the common people of the north show by their devotion to his great work that they agree with this high praise.

Nabha Das, a contemporary of TulsI Das, wrote the *Bhakta Mala,* or 'Garland of Devotees', a series of brief biographies of the chief *bhakti* saints.

Baby Rama in His Mother's Arms

With fingers locked in prayer she cries—How may I dare. O lord god immortal, thy boundless praise to tell?—

Far above the world's confusion and reason's vain intrusion, whom all the scriptures witness incomprehen-sible;

Whom saints and holy sages have hymned through all the ages, the fountain of compassion, the source of every grace;

Who aye with Lakshmi reignest, thou, even thou, now deignest to be my son and succour thy sore-tried chosen race.

Though we know by revelation, heaven and earth and all creation, in each hair upon thy body may be found,

In my arms thou sweetly dreamest, O mystery supremest, far beyond the comprehension of a sage the most profound.

Smiled the lord at her devotion, and would fain have set in motion the magic that dazzles the crowd,

Telling all he had done and the triumphs he had won, that his mother of her son might be proud.

But hurriedly she cried—' My soul is terrified by these marvels, disperse them from my sight;

Let me see thee as a child, disporting free and wild, for in this is my greatest delight.

She spoke and he obeyed, and, at once in fashion made, as an infant began to cry.

— Tulsi Das, *Ramacharit Manas*

FLAMBOYANT PILLARS IN DRVIDIAN TEMPLE

Krishnaites

The Krishnaite books in Sanskrit noticed earlier were followed up by some very interesting vernacular literature in the latter half of the fifteenth century. Vidyapati wrote many lyrics in the dialect of Bihar; Chandi Das did similar work in Bengali; and in Rajputana, MIra Bal, a princess, wrote beautiful songs, which are extremely popular, in the Braj Bhasha. This is the dialect of the country round Mathura, where Krishna's life among the cowherds is fabled to have been lived. In this very country the first fully systematized form of popular Krishnaism was founded in the early part of the sixteenth century by a Brahmin from the south named Vallabhacharya. In his teaching and among his followers the sensual elements which are present in all the later Krishnaite mythology come to the front and bear their harvest.

NORTHEN KRISHNAITE LEADERS

Century	*Name*	*Place*	*Works*	*Language*
XI	Nimbarka	....	....	....
XII	Jayadeva	Bengal	*Gita Govinda*	Sanskrit
XIII	Namdev	Maratha Land	Hymns	Marathi
XIV	....	....	....	....
XV	Vidyapati	Bihar	Sonnets	Maithili
	Chandi Das	Bengal	Songs	Bengali
	Mira Bai	Mewar	Songs	Braj
XVI	Vallabha	Mathura		
	Sur Das	Agra	*Sur Sagar*	Braj
	Chaitanya	Nadlya		Bengali
XVII	Tukaram	Maratha Land	*Abhanga,* hymns	Marathi

His son-in-law Chaitanya preached the faith of Krishna in Bengal, using the lyrics of Vidyapati to stir the emotions of the people. He was essentially a revivalist appealing to the feelings by music, singing, and devotional excitement. In his own time the nobler elements of the religion were in the ascendant; but soon immorality crept in and degraded the movement seriously. The most famous of Vallabhacharya's successors was Sur Das, the blind poet of Agra. His work is called the *Sur-Sagar,* and consists of exquisite songs on the legend of Krishna in the Braj dialect. Namdev and Tukaram, who were both Marathas, were Krishnaites. Tukaram's poems are greatly treasured.

The Praise of Krishna in Marathi

Krishna's Saving Power

What or whom shall we ask for but thee, O thou who fillest the globe and the universe? Who else knows how to fulfil our heart's desires? What of other princes and kings? There is none other in the three worlds that grants liberation, none that saves us but thou. When we think upon thy name and form, sin and fever run away in fear, desire is destroyed. Hari, this name of thine is truly called such in the PuraQas, for it drives away death and re-incarnation from those they have seized. Why should I waste my speech? It is fruitless for me to praise any other than thee. O thou that destroyest the world, the great serpent is wearied with describing thee. Let my spirit repose in confidence at thy feet; it is vain to ask for aught else. Thy title, 'Lord of the humble', is justified in the eyes of men; thou hast saved many a humble, many a guilty, many a sinful man. Tuka dwells at thy feet; preserve him, O God! I ask that I may serve thee.

Tukaram's Religious Experience

Step by step he supports me: my life is led on to perfection. I have found an assured place in him, and the world I have left void. My spirit goes forward on the path. I am filled in the flesh with growing joy. Tuka says, In this mortal world I have joined the pervading spirit.

—*Tukaram*

All the modern *Bhagavatas* reckon themselves to belong to one or other of four Mother-churches, though there are numerous subdivisions.

THE MODERN BHAGAVATAS

The four Churches	*Philosophic Position*	*Main Sect*	*Chief sub-sects*
		Ramaite	
I. SRI-SAMPRADAYA Founder: RAMANUJA	*Visishtadvaita,* Modified monism	Sri-sampradayas	I. Ramanandis 2. Kabirpanthis 3. Khakis 4. Muluk-dasis 5. Rai-dasis 6. Sena-panthis
II. BRAHMA-SAMPRADAYA Founder: MADHVA	*Dvaita,* Dualism	Madhvas	
		Krishnaite	
III. RUDRA-SAMRADAYA Founder: VISHNUSVAMI	*Suddkadvaita,* Pure monism	Vallabha-charis	I. Mira Bais 2. Chaitanyas
IV. SANAKADI-SAMPRADAYA Founder: NIMBARKA	*Dvaitadvaita,* Dualistic monism	Nimavats	I. Radha-Vallabhas 2. Charan-dasis 3. Sakhi-bhavas

Sampradaya means tradition. Thus Sri-sampradaya means the tradition handed down from Sri, i.e., Lakshmi, the wife

PICTURE FROM KABIR CHURA MONASTERY, BENARES

Surat Gopal and Dharm Das kneel in front of Kabir, while his son Kamal fans him.

of Vishnu. The second tradition is said to come from Brahma, the Creator, lhe third from Rudra, i.e., Siva, and the fourth from the sage Sanaka and his brethren.

Though both Ramaites, and Krishnaites accepted men of every caste as members of their sects, yet they never dreamed of doing away with caste.

Kabir

The deistic movement springs from Kabir, the weaver who was one of the apostles of Ramananda. Here Muhammedan influence makes itself distinctly felt. For, though KabIr was a disciple of Ramananda, though he calls God by the name Rama, and has Vedantic ideas, he will have nothing to do with the doctrine of incarnations, and **he condemns idolatry and caste with unsparing voice.** Yet he is recognised as an incarnation himself by his followers, the KabirpanthIs; and his polemic against caste has had but little effect: the Hindu and the Muhammedan members of his Church have separate monasteries and have little in common except their devotion to their Master and the Hindu members are almost all Sudras. **His pithy couplets and epigrammatic sayings are still very popular.** Dadu, a sixteenth-century cotton-cleaner of Ahmedabad, leader of the Dadupanthis, got his theology from Kabir.

The Kabirpanth

Its Leaders, Sects and Books

The *Bijak,* lit. 'the account book', a collection of hymns, of *Sakhis,* i.e., rhyming couplets, and short prose expositions of points of doctrine, published about 1570. Many of these re-appear in the *Adi Granth.* Multitudes of other *Sakhis* are current and are attributed to Kabir.

Kabir, died 1518

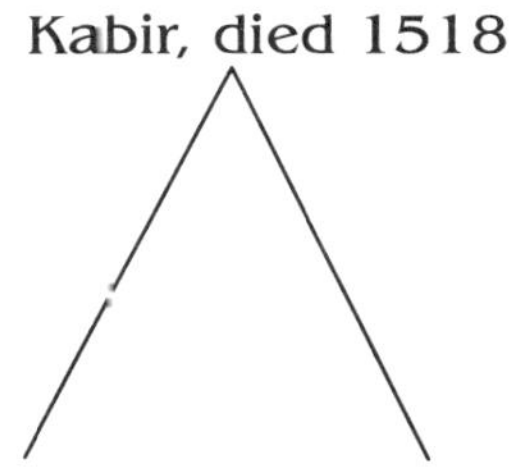

The Bap, i.e., Father, section at Kabir Chaura, Benares, and at Maghar, Gorakhpur District, where Kabir died. Founder: SURAT GOPAL.	The Mai, i.e., Mother, section at Chattisgarh, Founder: DHARM DAS	*Sukh Nidan,* a manual of doctrine published in 1729 *Amar Mul,* another manual of later origin.

Nanak

No direct Nanak influence exerted by Kabir, however, is equal to the indirect influence which has arisen through the founding of the Sikh sect in the Punjab by his disciple Nanak. From the beginning the chief guru of the church exercised large power; and the tenth guru, named Govind, took such steps as transformed the sect into a military order and finally created a great and warlike nation. But no guru succeeded Govind, and their sacred book, the *Granth,* is now the centre of the faith. It is a most interesting collection of varied material, some of it ordinary, some very valuable. Much of it was written by the gurus, but there are also hymns and sayings from all the great *bhakti* teachers of the north. The most important part, the *Adi Granth* or 'Original Book', was compiled by Guru Arjun in 1601. Govind Singh added. a great deal of new matter in 1696, and the whole is now called the *Granth.* **Nanak condemned idolatry, and Guru**

Govind abolished caste within the military order. Yet caste is now rife among the Sikhs; and the *Granth* is treated like an idol in their central shrine, the Golden Tempie of Amrltsar.

It is a most extraordinary fact that the theology of Kablr was meant to unite Hindus and Muhammedans in the worship of the one God; yet the most implacable hatred arose between the Sikhs and the Muhammedans; and **from that hatred came the Khalsa, the Sikh military order, which created the fiercest enemies the Mughal emperors had.** It is also most noteworthy that caste has found its way back into every Hindu sect that has disowned It.

THE BHAKTI PERIOD

External Events	*History*	*Religion*	*Literature*
1200		The Qutb Minar and Mosque built	Namdev Mey-kanda-devar
1300	1336 Vijayanagar founded		Umapati Madhva Sayana and Madhava
	1398 Taimur in India		
1400		Vidyapati Mira Bal	Ramananda Kabir
1500 Martin Luther	1526 the Mughals		Nanak
	1556 Akbar	Toleration	
1588 The Armada	1565 Battle of Talikot. Fall of Vijayanagar		Sur Das, Tulsl Das, Dadu, Chaitanya *Bhakta Mala*
1600		Intolerance renewed	1601 *Adi Granth*
Cromwell	1658 Aurangzeb		Tukaram 1696 *Granth*

Madhva

In the fourteenth century a new Vishnuite movement appeared at Udipi, in the Kannada country. The founder of the church is known as Madhvacharya, his followers as Srlmadhvas. Madhva was a sannyasi, and, like the other acharyas, he made his reputation by a commentary on the *Vedanta-Sutra.* His system is a dualism, and is frankly called *dvaita,* dualistic. If Ramanuja is farther from Sankara than Nilakantha, Madhva is still more distant. The sect of the Srimadhvas has attained considerable proportions and influence, especially in Western India. Later leaders produced hymns in so that there is an opportunity for popularizing the doctrine. But Madhva was much more exclusive than either the Saivas or the followers of Ramanuja. **He laid great stress on caste, on cleanliness of person and clothes, and on temple ritual. Krishna was his favourite divinity.**

Saiva

In the thirteenth and fourteenth centuries the Saivas of the south developed their teaching into a philosophical system which is called the *Saiva Siddhanta,* and which is expressed in a series of Tamil books, partly in verse, partly in prose. The teachers who produced this vernacular literature received the title acharya.

Tamil Literature of Saiva Siddhanta

A. The twelve canonical books, called *Tirumurai* or *Dravida Sruti:*

Cent.	*Authors*	*Books*	
VII	Appar		3
	Nana Sambandhar	The *Devaram*	3
VIII	Sundarar		1
X	Manikka Vachakar	*Tiruvachakam* and *Tirukovaiyar*	1
	Nine authors:	*Tiruvisaipa*	1
	Tirumular:	*Tirumantram*	1
	Nambi-andar-nambi		1
	Sekkilar	*Periya Puramam*	1
			12

B. The fourteen *Siddhanta Sastras.* Of these the most important are:

XIII	Mey-kanda-devar	*Siva-nana-bodham,* a systematic statement of the principles of the faith, translated from the *Raurava Agama*
	Mana-vachakam Kadandar	*Unmai Vilakkam*
	Arunandi-devar	*Siva-nana-siddhi,* a further exposition
XIV	Umapati Sivacharyar	*Siva Prakasam,* a poem in a hundred quatrains, being a commentary on the two preceding works *Tiru-arut-payan,*a poem in a hundred couplets on divine grace

Adoration Mantras

(a) Bhagavata:

Om namo Bhagavate Vasudevaya, 'Om! reverence to the adorable Vasudeva.'

(b) Early Buddhist:

Om namo Bhagavate, 'Om! reverence to the Adorable.'

(c) Later Buddhist:

Namo mitabhaya, 'Reverence to Amitabha.'

(d) The five syllables of the Saiva Siddhanta, *Sivaya namah,* 'Reverence to Siva.'

(e) The followers of Ramanuja:

Om namo Narayanaya, 'Om! reverence to Narayana.'

(f) The followers of Ramananda:

Om Ramaya namah, 'Om! reverence to Rama.'

(g) The Vallabhacharis:

Sri Krishna Saranam mama, 'Holy Krishna is my refuge.'

Muhammedan influence touched Hindus effectively in another direction. Partly in self-defence, partly in imitation of their masters, the upper classes of **Hindu society began to seclude their women: the zenana system dates from Muhammadan times.** Like other high-class customs, It is copied by the lower classes so far as their means will allow.

The Literature of the Saivas and the Vaishnavas

This table is meant to give some idea of the strikingly parallel development which these sects have had in South India. Both acknowledge the Vedas, though there are certain sections of them which they hold in less honour than their own literature. Both sects acknowledge to the full the inspiration and authority of the *Vedanta-sutra.*

The following are the chief divisions of their respective literatures:

	Saivas	Vaishnavas
1. Basal works in Sanskrlt verse taking the place of Srauta-sutras and the Karma-mimamsa	The Agamas or Saivagamas	The Samhitas or Pancharatra Samhitas
2. Tamil Hymns by early saints	The *Devaram.* 01 the three Adiyars and Manikka Vachakar's works	The *Nalayira Prabandham* of the Alvars
3. Commentary in Sanskrit prose on the *Vedanta-sutra*	The *Saiva Bhashya* of NiIakal,	The *Sri Bhashya* of Ramanuja
4. Philosophic works in Tamil	The fourteen Siddhanta Sutras	The *Artha Panchaka* of Pillai Lokacharya and other books

Hinduism Now

When the British conquered India, Hindu society was in a mess owing to historical factors. Long centuries of Muslim oppression had unnerved its constituents, including religion. The period after Aurangzeb was confusion worse confounded, but the Maratha and Sikh efforts were trying to push up resurgence and revival in a most vigorous manner.

The sudden intervention of the British in the form of traders had injected an unexpected and unusual element in the country's life, which was good as well as bad at the same time. It enslaved the country as also freed it and gave it new ideas, including railways, factories, postal system, etc. Christianity came with them, which worked both ways, on the one hand, condemning the Hindu religion and practices most severely in order to convert the people as soon as they could, as they and their compatriots had been doing in other parts of the world; and on the other, being themselves influenced by the fineries of Hindu philosophy, which no other country had done to them. This in turn inspired the Hindus themselves to slart their own renaissance and revive the country after over a thousand years.

The story of Sir William Jones in Calcutta, and the pro-Hindu culture movement started by him in that city, by learning Sanskrit and by founding the Royal Asiatie Society for studies and researches, is rather well known. Scholars from not only Britain but Germany — the largest number from any one country — France, Italy, Holland, Russia, pushed through Sanskrit, Pali and other literature to discover knowledge they had never heard of. Max Muller, Paul Deussen, Macdonald, Rhys Davids, Farquhar, etc., the list is too long to be noted here. Sanskrit became the rage of scholarly studies, it had cast new light on Euro-Asian history and had given birth to the new sciences of Linguistics and, later on, Philology. Max Muller, the ardent Christian, edited and published the 50 large volumes of the 'Sacred Books of the East' with the help of a bevy of scholars. He was deputed by the East India Company to prepare ground to Christianise India, but he ended up by writing 'What India Can Teach Us', as well as a short life of Ramakrishna Paramahansa.

The process was not new, it had started long ago. Dara Shikoh, Aurangzeb's elder brother, had got sixty Upanishads translated into Persian in the seventeenth century itself, which somehow reached Greece and drew the attention of two scholars, who both re-translated these into Latin and had them published. Destiny played its part once again and Anquetil Duperron's translations fell in the hands of the famous French philosopher, Arthur Schopenhauer. He was so enthralled by the high philosophy of the Upanishads that he started promoting it in the West rather vehemently. The new studies and publications of Sanskrit literature were the next, and a very major effort in that already established direction.

A religio-cultural renaissance in India started in right earnest in India. Its first major expression was in Bengal, where the British had concentrated and were active in the academic areas, too. Raja Rammohan Roy started the first movement known as the Brahmo Samaj which promoted a simpler worship influenced by Christianity. Keshav Chandra Sen, Debendranalh Tagore and others came up with new ideas and practices, creating a fermentation unknown till then. The Raja also got the practice of Sati outlawed in the country, a groundbreaking contribution to social reform. Rabindranath Tagore, son of Debendranath Tagore, further expanded the awakening through new literature, drama, music and education, by establishing the grand multisided experiment, Santiniketan; he won the Nobel Prize in 1913, the first in Asia — which added further laurels to Indian culture and made its high points known to the whole world.

The second great movement was initiated by Swami Dayanand of Gujerat, who established the Arya Samaj in 1875, promoting perhaps the most enlightened arm of Hinduism, decrying the rampant idolatry and temple-worship, declaring that the Vedas did not approve of it. He was a great fighter who fought singlehanded the temple worshipper Sanatanis and those forcibly converting the Hindus, the Muslims and Christians. He provided a near complete agenda for India's change and his movement spread like wild fire in north India, contributing substantially to the slowly emerging freedom movement also. It provided revolutionaries with revolvers as well as non-violent brigades of Gandhi. Its DAV schools and colleges spread a right mix of the ancient and modern education in a big way, and remain the largest education group in the country till date.

Another movement known as Prarthana Samaj was launched in Bombay and it spread in Maharashtra, with Mahadev Govind Ranade as its leader. Its contribution to women's awakening was remarkable. But South India did not witness any major tranformation though the Theosophical Society started by Madame Blavatsky of Russia in New York in 1975, shifted its headquarters to Madras (now Chennai) because it gave the greatest importance to Hindu religion, but its overemphasis on secret communications with the Tibetan masters, and later on, on announcing a world liberator or messiah in the form of J. Krishnamurti

— who instead of accepting the honour, repudiated it openly — made it lose its ground and possible contribution to world religion. But its second major leader Annie Besant did contribute something quite substantial to India's freedom by her society known as the Home Rule League and by joining the freedom movement led by Gandhi.

Yet another major movement developed in Bengal with the emergence of Ramakrishna Paramahansa whose simple ways and devotional teaching made him very popular, and whose disciple, Vivekananda, won over the American intellectual world by appearing and speaking in the Parliament of Religions at Chicago in 1893. Though quite young at the time, he was an excellent speaker and his scholarship in religious matters was remarkable, He promoted a world religion based on Vedanta which, it is important to note, attracted attention of many western intellectuals, and some of whom got ready to work for it — and taught Raja Yoga to them, for the first time. But he didn't live long, passing away without reaching 40 and, with his demise his great agenda dissolved into thin air. His organisation and the vast group of disciples found it convenient to forget his main task and promises. But it should be underlined that Vivekananda's striking work did start a new chapter in present day Hinduism. While he lived, he walked like a collosus in America and Europe and in his own country and spoke like a Vyasa.

He was a thinker also, an idea he left in seed form was taken up a decade later by Cambridge-returned revolutionary Aurobindo Ghose — later on famous as Sri Aurobindo — who tried to translate it into reality — a forty years' long yogic experiment which he carried out staying in one simple home in Pondicherry. The idea was that with yoga the next state of human evolution could be acquired. To achieve the objective, he devised a new form of yoga and called it Purna Yoga, or Integral Yoga. A French yoga-practitioner Mira Alfassa by name, joined him in the unusual experiment; she became famous all over the world as The Mother. The news that the new species might take birth at Pondicherry shook the intellectuals in the West and many started flocking to the Ashrama to participate in it.

It was a tremendous movement of its own kind — the present writer was also interested; though very young then, he penned perhaps the first Hindi book, a short one, on Sri Aurobindo's life and his great experiment. But nothing came out of it all, and suddenly the spiritual scientist passed away. I was at the time working as a journalist with a daily newspaper edited by a later-to-be prime minister of the country, Atal Behari Vajpayee; and one late evening when the news flashed on the teleprinter, repeating every five minutes, I was shocked out of my senses — one I would never forget and could revive at a second's notice.

Had the experiment failed? No one knows. It may perhaps succeed after a passage of time. The Mother tried several other ways to make the higher consciousness descend into human mind and body structure, but in vain. But the idea does have potential and is likely to take some kind of life. We may keep our fingers crossed.

The first half of the twentieth century was the period dominated by Tilak, Gokhale and Gandhi, and also Subhas– of these Gandhi was a giant, a political experimenter in non-violence. He won freedom for India, greatly influenced the whole world, but was killed in the first year of independence. The second half of the century is now past and the country is struggling to stand on its own feet. Hinduism is speading as a better religious option in the West, ably assisted by Buddhistic ideas, and their philosophy of tolerance. In India Christianity is also being Hinduised, not only in ritual but also in its ideology that other religions may also be true — much to the chagrin of the Pope.

But Islam is not being contained either in India or abroad. Gandhi's failure in this area had resulted in his killing. In India it has resulted in the partition of the country, resulting in enormous bloodshed; and in the immediate present, it is terrorising the whole world. This is a story of gore, unparalleled in history. The West which has in its initial stages — they were responsible for the partition of India also — given it a supporting hand, is now fighting tooth and nail against it. The 9/11 incident in New York — an unexpected attack of unbelievable form and magnitude — has finally, though not sufficiently, succeeded in changing their policies to an extent.

But it seems that India again is taking the lead. Some enlightened Muslim groups, the Devbandis of north India in particular, are organising a regular movement against terrorism perpetrated by Muslims, declaring quite emphatically that Islam does not support it. (They had also opposed the partition of India.) Sections of Muslims have realised the futility of terrorism and are turning to peace and tolerance. How far will they be able to go? ... Anyway, India shows the way once again.

This is the general scenario of modern Hinduism. There has been a successful renaissance, and we are now 'marketing' — is this the correct word? — our achievements. There have been our Yogananda, Osho, Maharishi Mahesh Yogi, Swami Prabhupada, Swami Muktananda, Satya Sai Baba and others, and despite some of their failings, we are making our mark in the market of spiritual ideas in the world. In comparision to the rest, our ideas are the best, standing well in the test of time, and the only hope for a better world, a global one, which is slowly but surely emerging. Our ideal since our earliest days has been *Vasudhaiva Kutumbakam* — The World Is One Family.

Select Scriptures

Perennial Philosophy
— Annie Besant

•

Seeds:
From the Rigveda

•

Branches:
Some Upanishads

•

Flowers:
The Essential Gita

Perennial Philosophy

A religion can only be understood by sympathy; it can only be expounded by the speaker placing himself for the time being in the heart of that religion and showing it forth as it would appear to its most devoted and learned adherents. The first of the great religions with which I am to deal is that known under the name of Hinduism, a religion which is the religion of the majority in this country and which had its cradle in the northern part of this land.

The Aryan race — the first family of its stock from which others were later to spring — that which in modern times we speak as Hindu but that always in the early days was called Aryan — was settled in the north of India in the region between the Himalayas and the Vindhyas, known as Aryavarta, and there gradually evolved along definite lines laid down for it by its Manu and by those who surrounded him.

The whole civilization is religious, and there is nothing in human life regarded as 'secular' or 'profane'. The intellect has been encouraged to exert itself freely, as witness the schools of thought comprised under the all-embracing 'Hinduism'; but right conduct as it affects the social fabric has ever been rigidly enforced. Freedom of opinion, but orthodoxy in life, have been characteristic of Hinduism throughout its long evolution: hence the vast range and diversity of philosophies, and the stability of its social fabric and its family life. A Hindu may think as he will about God — as one with the universe, separate from the universe — or may even exclude Him entirely.

Our subject falls naturally into three divisions: (l) the spiritual truths, with their later intellectual presentations; these are given in the Vedas and in the Upanishads which are an integral part of them. We have in the Vedas a complete presentation of spiritual truth, not fully expressed but implicitly contalned, so that it is written that Brahman is concealed in the Upanishads as the Upanishads are concealed in the Vedas. Gradually this was to be expressed In the course of evolution; a perfect whole was given to be unfolded as time went on. This was the higher knowledge *(vidya)* — the knowledge of Brahman — and the lesser *vidya* comprised the *Vedangas,* the sixty-four sciences which codified the knowledge of nature, and the methods of gaining knowledge, a mine of gold from which might now be dug out scientific lore that would set the modern world a-wondering.

Then comes (2) the exoteric cult, detailed and wonderfully minute in its delineation of Nature and of man's relation to it, with the Puranas as its popular expression, with the ordinances linking it to the outer social and family conduct. Later on, we find book after book, the *Ramayana* and the *Mahabharata.*

Varieties of opinion about God are valuable, not mischievous, because each opinion by itself expresses so small a fragment of the mighty truth, and the totality of opinions gives a fuller presentation than could otherwise be gained. But conduct covers all man's relations to external nature, visible and invisible, and according to his conduct harmony or discord accrues.

We now come to (3) the science of yoga by which alone spiritual truths can be fully realised, by the gradual unfolding of the inner faculties which enable man to study the invisible world directly, and by expansion of his consciousness to embrace wider and subtler ranges of being. The truths given in the Vedas were to be realised by yoga, but its methods are nowhere fully stated. To this end was the guru instituted, that he might teach the worthy pupil to tread this difficult path, sharp as the edge of a razor.

A true knowledge of spiritual truths can only be obtained by yoga that, there is a science of the soul which is taught by the guru, and which enables a man, step by step, to rise to the highest spiritual wisdom.

Let us glance at the beginning of the universe, the commencement of manifestation, when Brahman, the Self of the universe, manifests himself in order that the universe may be. It is written: 'When He is mamfest, all is manifested after Him; by His manifestation this all becomes manifest.'[1] How he comes into manifestation we know not, but we are told that it is by an act of sacrifice: 'Om! the dawn in truth is the head of the sacrificial horse.'[2]

Occult wisdom teaches that this act of sacrifice is the self-limitation of Brahman, his circumscribing of himself by maya, i.e., by *avidya.*[3] Without this no universe could be manifest, since limitation is necessary to variety, and each thing is enveloped in *avidya,* that is, is limited, is shut out from being all else, from being perfect knowledge.

With Brahman the manifested universe begins; he is the source, the fount, the one Self, and the one breath of the universe; outside him is nothing that is manifest, outside him there is no life, no thought, no mind. Manifesting in his threefold attributes, he is *sat, chit, ananda,* and from him all qualities come forth. He enfolds these in one, the First, the Cause of all.

---

1. *Mundakopanishad,* 2.2.10
2. *Brihadaranyakopanishad,* 1.1.1
3. Maya is illusion, all that is changing, transitory, in contrast to the permanent Reality, the One Life. Therefore, it is the root of matter, matter being that which takes form and adapts itself to the impulses of the life it clothes. *Avidya,* absence of knowledge, is another name for it.

That Brahman, that mighty One, the Self of the universe, is descnbed in a passage of wonderful beauty and sublimity in the *Svetasvataropanishad:*

'When there is no darkness, neither day nor night, neither being nor non-beIng, there is only that supremely Auspicious One, ever alone. He is indestructible. He is to be adored by the creator *Savitra.* From him alone comes forth the ancient wisdom. Not above, nor below, nor in the midst can he be comprehended, nor is there any similitude for him whose name is infInite glory. Not by the sight is established his form: none beholds him by the eye. Those who know him by the heart and the mind, dwelling in the heart, become immortal.' (4. 18-20)

Then coming to the manifested universe, where some knowledge is possible to us. we learn that the manifestation of Brahman is gradual and not sudden, and that all comes forth from him not at once but slowly.

As salt in the water in which it is dissolved,[1] as fire in the wood before the fire sticks are rubbed together, as butter in the milk that is brought forth by churning,[2] as cream in clarified butter,[3] so is Brahman concealed as the Self of every creature. Stage after stage the marvels of his manifestation; stage by stage the might of his unfolding; his quality of *sat,* of pure existence, comes forth in the unmoving creation, in the mineral kingdom, where existence only can be said to be shown. *Chit* and *ananad* are there concealed, and only *sat* is manifest. Then in the vegetable world the unfolding life shows us the beginning of pleasure and pain, the germ which develops into *ananda* in the later stages of evolution; and in the animal world

1. *Chhandogyopanishad,* 6. 14
2 *Svetasvataropanishad,* 1. 16
3 Ibid., 4. 16

there is shown forth also the germ of *chit,* which is to have its later and fuller evolution; and in man the germs partially manifested of *sat, chit* and *ananda* until at the end of the evolution *sat, chit* and *ananda* are perfectly developed in him. Then he is Brahman; he has become one.

All this is wrought by the slow course of evolution, by birth after birth, by death after death, by that wheel of births and deaths which turns unceasingly in the three worlds. The lowest world — the world of our waking consciousness — is *bhur-loka* (this earth). There man is born in the physical body, there he gathers experience by coming into contact with material objects; then through the gateway of death he passes into the next world *bhuvar-loka* (the astral world) and in a body suited to that world he works out a part of the experience made upon the earth. Then in a third body, ascending to *svarga-loka* (Devachan), he works out the fruit of others of his earthly experiences. From *svarga-loka* he returns again through *bhuvar-loka* to the gateway of birth, to *bhur-loka,* there to begin again his learning, the fruits of which he assimilates in the other worlds.

To this wheel man is bound by desire, by the thirst for sentient existence, which in his ignorance he identifies at first with the life of the body. 'This *Purusha* (inner man) has the nature of desire. As is his desire so is his resolve; as is his resolve so is his work; as is his work so is his reward. He who is attached obtains by means of work the object to which his mind, as the cause, is attached. Having arrived at the last effect (in *svarga)* of the work which he here performs, he comes from that world again to this world in consequence of his work. Thus he who desires wanders from world to world ... When all desires dwelling in the heart have been abandoned, then the mortal becomes immortal.'[1] Ceasing to identify himself with the body, he

---

1. *Brihadaranyakopanishad,* 4. 4. 5-7

identifies himself with the mind, and then merely lives for a longer time in *svarga,* still bound by desire. Freedom from rebirth only comes when desire is dead to anything the three worlds have to give.

Next, all this evolution proceeds under the law of causation, each cause working out its due effect. This is the law of karma that returns to every man exactly the results of his sowing. He sows his karma in the world of physical matter, he reaps it partially in the other two worlds and there assimilates the results of his thinking. Then he returns to earth, the creature of his own making, to work out karma belonging to this earth. So he grows life after life, being 'a creature of reflection; what he reflects on in this life he becomes the same hereafter'.[1]

In this way he climbs from stage to stage with ever-expanding consciousness, sheath after sheath developing within him, and each one a vehicle of consciousness. As he develops, he expands his consciousness to embrace one world after another — the stages of consciousness corresponding to those three worlds being the stages of *jagrat, svapna* and *sushupti.*[2]

Consciousness expands, embracing each world in turn, until man is the master and sovereign where at first he was the child and the student. Then rising yet higher, he escapes from the wheel of births and deaths; he passes from the body of the moon[3] as it is technically called, into the body

---

1. *Chhandogyopanishad,* 3. 14. 1

2. Consciousness is a unit, but it may work in the *jagrat* state, i.e., in the physical body, in *bhur-loka;* in the *svapna* state, i.e., in the astral body, in *bhuvar-loka;* or in the *sushupti* state, i.e., in the mental body, in *svarga-loka.* Hence *jagrat* is called the waking-consciousness; *svapna* the dream-consciousness; and *sushupti* the dreamless-sleep consciousness. The English names are misleading unless the facts are understood.

3. The astral and lower mental bodies.

of the sun[1], and when this is completely mastered, he comes back no more to enforced birth. Rising to the *turiya* state he attains the Self, clad in *anandamaya-kosa.*[2]

Such, roughly sketched, are the essentials of that philosophy of Hinduism by which man is taught something of the spiritual truths that underlie evolution. All this will be done by humanity life after life. But what all men will do in the course of countless ages, a man may do, if he will by greater effort, by intenser exertion, by means of that science of yoga which trains the soul more swiftly than the ordinary evolution.

Evolution is but the will of Isvara showing itself in the manifested universe; borne on the stream of evolution, humanity is carried onwards to its goal. But the strong swimmer may reach the goal more swiftly than a floating straw; by yoga a man may finish his journey while yet the mass of humanity is floating slowly along with the current of evolution.

Attempts to bring down this wonderful thought to the region of intellect gave birth to the **six great schools of Indian philosophy**, with all their countless modifications. Every school of Hindu philosophy seeks liberation from the limits of painful existence, from the miseries of birth and death. All admit that the divine knowledge, brahma-vidya, is necessary for this freedom; they differ in the way they express their goal and in the methods they employ to reach it. The schools fall readily into three pairs, characterized by their fundamental view of the universe and by their way of proof.

First we have those founded on the **atomic theory**; these are the two schools known as the **Nyaya** of Gautama

---

1. The higher mental and causal bodies.
2. The buddhic or bliss body.

and the **Vaiseshika** of Kanada, which have also very much in common in their methods of research. They seek knowledge by way of inference, by logical process, dividing everything into categories, considering the nature of proof, the nature of inference — the very essence of the mind worked out in fullest details, based on the atomic theory and **developed along the lines of pure reason**. They remain as monuments of pure intellect, remarkable not only for the perfection with which the reasoning is conducted, but also for the training they give to the mind. The nature of things is sought into and, in order that error may be avoided, there is the keenest analysis of the tools by which the investigation is to be made.

Then we come to the two schools which are built on the duality of the manifested universe, on the co-eternity of the two fundamentals, never disjointed, ever interworking, a cosmogony of the most logical coherence being worked out in linked succession. These are the **Samkhya** of Kapila, sometimes called the atheistic Samkhya because it does not go behind the dual manifestation, and the **yoga** of Patanjali, or the theistic Samkhya.

In the first, the fundamental duality of the manifested universe is the starting point. ***Purusha,*** Spirit, or rather the multitude of individual *purushas,* is regarded as eternal, and ***Prakriti,*** or matter, is regarded as co-eternal with them. Prakriti is threefold, showing **sattva**, ***rajas*** and ***tamas*** as its three *gunas* and is full of activities, but it is aimless and can do nothing save as clothing Purusha. Hence the favourite simile, that Purusha is like a lame man with good eyes carried on the shoulders of a blind man with good legs; the two together can walk and avoid stumbling into pitfalls.

Then follows the working out of the whole manifested universe, under the heads of **twenty-five *tattvas* or**

principles, as we may call them, deduced with keen insight, with logical precision, with the most careful observation of facts, so that, taken as a cosmogony limited to the manifested universe, the Samkhya may be said ever to hold its own. The Yoga of Patanjali accepts the Samkhya cosmogony as it stands, but adds to it the **twenty-sixth *tattva*, Isvara**, the deity to be worshipped. For Patanjali truly said that **without a form the mind could not concentrate itself in meditation**, and he sought knowledge not by investigation into the universe along the Samkhyan lines, but by the suppression of the modifications of the thinking principle; those modifications were regarded as barriers between the thinker and the One that he sought. Only when the mind was one-pointed could man escape from this limitation.

Lastly, we have the two great Mimamsa schools — the **Purva Mimamsa** and the **Uttara Mimamsa**. In the first, the system of Jaimini, we have rites, ceremonies, all that is the outer part of a man's religious life, dealt with and expounded with the greatest minuteness. The Uttara Mimamsa is the **Vedanta, the best known perhaps in the West of these six great Indian schools**. This is divided into three sub-schools, the **Dvaita**, **Visishtadvaita** and the **Advaita**. They accept the Samkhya cosmogony on the course of the evolution of the manifested universe, but are not satisfied to stop where the Samkhya stops. The Vedanta — the 'end of the Veda' — seeks the cause of the manifested universe, cannot rest content with an analysis that stops at *Purusha* and *Prakriti*. It is, in fact, the most splendid philosophical expression of that ineradicable yearning of the human heart for God. It may be denied, distorted, thwarted, but ever rises from its seeming death, the eternal witness of man's innermost Self, his inalienable life that finds its noblest outcome in the triumph cry of the Advaitin, 'I am He!' when the long-sought under many veils is found, and Deity stands revealed as the very Self of man.

The three sub-schools of the Vedanta should be regarded as successive steps, rather than as opposing theories; all assert the divine existence as the source of the universe, but the Dvaita teaching alleges an eternal division between God and man — they remain eternally distinct. The Visishtadvait goes a step further, asserting duality but merging it into a final unity. The Advaita insists on the fundamental unity, and is so intent on this that — dazzled by the darkness that is 'excess of light' — it well-nigh loses sight of the universe, seeing only the One under the illusive forms. But when from intellectual disquisition he rises into devotion, the Advaita Vedantin also recognises the manifestation of Brahman in the gods, and where can we find such fervid intensity of rapt devotion as in the hymns to **Siva** and to **Durga of that chief of Advaita Vedantins**, **Sri Sankaracharya**?

In the Advaita is the familiar teaching as to Maya, the illusion-causing power of Divine Thought — the universe but the thought of the One without a second. All but Brahman is illusion, limited, transient, ever-changing; the One that is permanent is the only reality. All that changes is illusory; the manifestation is but a thought.

Perhaps that idea, diffcult to grasp, may be made clearer if we remember that the human mind can also by its thought impose illusions on another mind that is under its control. When a man is hypnotised, he can be made to feel the resistance of a body, to see it, to hear it, to touch it and smell it — to have every record of senses by which we guide our outer life complete — and yet there is nothing there but the thought of the hypnotiser who imposes all these sensations directly on the mind. The moment the man is dehypnotised the illusion vanishes, and he knows nothing is there.

Similarly, in this view the universe is but God's thought expressed and dominating the whole for all forms are but thoughts of God. When that is once realised, the One is seen and the separation and the difference disappear. Sheath after sheath of *avidya* is stripped off the Self; sheath after sheath is pierced through by the eye of wisdom, until the seer declares that: 'In the highest golden sheath is spotless, partless Brahman. THAT, the true light of lights, known to the knowers of the Self.[1] But before man knows it, he wanders about in the universe of forms, yet that which really attracts him in every form is not the phenomenal appearance but the Self which shines within it.

We love forms because the Self is in them; we are attracted by forms because a broken ray of the light of the Self shines through. As the child sees the pebble shining on the road after rain and goes to pick it up, attracted not by the dull bit of earth but by the light of the sun which is reflected from it, so do all men — even in their vices — deluded by outer appearance, follow the broken light of Self. That is what they are groping after, but in their blindness they fail to understand, they do not realise.

All persons too are loved for the Self within them. 'Not for the sake of the wife, the wife is dear but for the sake of the Self the wife is dear; not for the sake of the husband is the husband dear, but for the sake of the Self is the husband dear;' and so on with one thing after another in the manifested universe, until at last we say: 'Not for the sake of the gods the gods are dear, but for the sake of the Self the gods are dear.'[2]

---

1. Mundakopanishad, 2, 2, 9.

2. Brihadaranyakopanishad, 4, 5, 6.

Thus man rises from stage to stage, ever coming nearer to the Self; thus it is that first he realizes division — 'I am I, Thou art Thou, Thou art to be adored, Thou art to be worshipped, I am Thy *bhakta,* Thy devotee.' Drawing nearer and nearer to the vision of light, there comes a dawning sense of likeness, the lover and the beloved cannot be really two; until at last, with love made perfect and wisdom no longer stained by ignorance, the lover and the beloved merge in one: 'I am He!' and there is unity where duality reigned before.

From this you can probably see why it was that in the old days the teaching of the Vedanta was not given to the world at large. The path of the unmanifested, says Sri Krishna, 'is hard for the embodied to reach'. Through the embodied we rise to the unembodied, through forms to the formless. Therefore, Sri Sankaracharya laid it down as a preparation for learning the Advaita that the man should evolve in himself certain qualifications, and until those were evolved the Advaita was never taught. How wise and necessary was this restriction: we see the evil use to which this noble teaching is put today by men with uncontrolled senses and untrained minds.

We have arrived at the next division of our subject — the **science of Yoga**, the way by which a man may hasten his evolution, expand his consciousness, and rise into union with the Supreme. Yoga was the final stage of an evolution patiently trodden with ever-increasing recognition of the goal, from the worship of the lower devatas through the four asramas up to the direct training for the liberation of the soul from the wheel of births and deaths.

There are three paths, and each has its own yoga. ***Karma-marga,*** the final stage of which is ***karma-yoga;*** ***Jnana-marga,*** leading to ***Jnana-yoga; Bhakti-marga,*** ending with ***Bhakti-yoga.*** For all of them, the subdual of senses and control of mind are essential prerequisites, but the methods to accomplish this differ with the paths.

In the *karma-marga* a man learns by constant practice in daily life. In the home he practises restraint of the senses, is self-denying, self-sacrificing. He gains control of the mind by his daily meditation, by accuracy and diligence in his business, by utilising the constant opportunities of maintaining concentration and balance amid the distractions and the whirl of the common life of men.

When by lives of such effort he has prepared himself, he begins the *karma-yoga* by which he learns to perform action as duty, without desire for fruit ('renouncing the fruits of action,' as it is called). He performs every duty with scrupulous fidelity, but he renounces all results. Finally, he performs every action as sacrifice to the Supreme, his only motive, the doing of the will of Isvara.

By this, though living in the world, he has no attachments, and is at heart the unattached, the wanderer. By this, he builds his 'hut' and has his solitary place for meditation. By this, he realizes the pure 'I' and its unity with other 'I's and is the *hamsa.* By this, he rises above the 'I' and becomes the *paramahamsa.*[1] By renunciation and sacrifice, *ahamkara*[2] is destroyed, and with its destruction the blinding veils fall away from his eyes and he is filled with *jnana* and *bhakti,* for the end of the three paths is one.

For the *jnana-marga* a man develops his intellect by study pursued through many lives, until he has reached a point at which he begins to weary of mere knowledge and seeks the permanent truth of which all knowledge is but a part. Then he must develop *viveka,* discrimination between

1. These stages are described in the *Jnana-marga*
2. The quality of I-ness, separateness

the real and the unreal; *vairagya,* disgust for the unreal; *shatsampatti,* the six mental qualifications - *sama,* control of the mind; *dama,* control of the body; *uparati,* broad-minded tolerance; *titiksha,* endurance; *sraddha,* faith; *samadhana,* balance; he must have *mumuksha,* the longing for liberation from the transitory. Then, with all these, he is the *adhikarin,* the man fitted to receive initiation into Yoga.[1]

Then he follows the *jnana-yoga,* and discerning the valuelessness of the transitory, he becomes the *parivrajaka* — the wanderer unattached by desire, the homeless man. By yet deeper vision, he realises the permanent, and rests on that as his secure foundation, so becoming the *kutichara,* the dweller in the hut, abiding in that one secure resting-place.

Then he feels the self-consciousness clearly, realises the 'I', and sees the same 'I' in others, the Hamsa stage. Rising above it, as the spiritual vision is clarified and consciousness expands, he becomes the Parama-hamsa, beyond the 'I', and realizes 'I am He'.

Bhakti-marga is trodden by the soul whose affections are drawn towards some manifested aspect of God. Its early stages are those of devoted worship, of deep love and reverence. Gradually the soul takes on the qualities it worships, becoming that which it adores. The non-attachment gained by renunciation in *karma-marga,* by discrimination in *jnana-marga,* it gains by expelling all lower attachments by the one attachment to its Lord. By love it conquers all baser desires, and they wither for lack of expression; sacrifice is a joyful acting out of devotion.

---

1. These were the qualifications laid down by Sri Sankaracharya before a man was allowed to study Vedanta, for the Vedanta cannot be realised without Yoga.

Each of the four stages is trodden with love, as the active means of accomplishment, until the love that the worshipper finds the object of its worship embracing it, and feels itself merging into complete unity with its Beloved.

In truth the three paths blend, and in the higher stages one cannot be separated from the other; for the *karma-yogin* is full of bhakti, and also by his sacrifice destroys *ahamkara* and thus becomes perfect in wisdom. The *jnanin* and the *bhakta* each takes on the qualities of the other. In the heart of the *bhakta* wisdom arises spontaneously, and in the heart of the *jnanin, bhakti* flowers as the inevitable result of vision.

In the later stages of each path, as soon as his services are needed, the Guru appears, and takes the soul under his guidance; the man becomes a *sishya*. The guru does not come to the unprepared, the unready, though the impatience of man often cries out for his presence when that presence would be unheeded were it there. He leads the soul through the later stages, giving such adjusting aid as is required, helping it to unfold the divine potentialities within it, thus hastening its evolution until achievement is reached.

Then the disciple in his turn, becomes the liberated soul, ready and fit to help onwards the less advanced. He becomes the *jivanmukta* living in the body still, a link between physical humanity and spiritual humanity, a channel of divine love and strength to man. Or he may become the *videhamukta,* living in the invisible world, still yielding service to the One, still carrying out the divine purpose, serving in other ways as a channel of spiritual life to men. These mighty ones pay their debts to their own gurus by service of the present and of the future *sishyas,* just as they received their own illumination from gurus developed in the past. Thus universe succeeds universe, each aiding its successors until our thought fails to express itself, and the human faculty sinks down unable to soar further.

SEEDS:
From the Rigveda

Kah : Who?

Hiranyagarbha

Kah (qius) meaning Who? that is, the Unknown God, has been applied as a name to Prajapati, and to other gods.

1. In the beginning rose Hiranyagarbha, born Only Lord of all created beings.

   He fixed and holdeth up this earth and heaven.
   What God shall we adore with our oblation?

2. Giver of vital breath, of power and vigour, he whose commandments all the Gods acknowledge:

   The Lord of death, whose shade is life immortal.
   What God shall we adore with our oblation?

3. Who by his grandeur hath become Sole Ruler of all the moving world that breathes and slumbers;

   He who is Lord of men and Lord of cattle.
   What God shall we adore with our oblation?

4. His, through his might, are these snowcovered mountains, and men call sea and Rasa his possession:

   His arms are these, his are these heavenly regions.
   What God shall we adore with our oblation?

5. By him the heavens are strong and earth is steadfast, by him light's realm and sky-vault are supported:

By him the regions in mid air were measured.
What God shall we adore with our oblation?

6. To him, supported by his help, two armies embattled look while trembling in their spirit,

   When over them the risen Sun is shining.
   What God shall we adore with our oblation?

7. What time the mighty waters came, containing the universal germ, producing Agni,

   Thence sprang the Gods' one spirit into being.
   What God shall we adore with our oblation?

8. He in his might surveyed the floods containing productive force and generating Worship.

   He is the God of gods, and none beside him.
   What God shall we adore with our oblation?

9. Ne'er may he harm us who is earth's Begetter, nor he whose laws are sure, the heavens' Creator,

   He who brought forth the great and lucid waters.
   What God shall we adore with our oblation?

10. Prajapati! thou only comprehend all these created things, and none beside thee.

    Grant us our hearts' desire when we invoke thee:
    may we have store of riches in possession.

(X/21)

SRISHTI: CREATION

Prajapati

1. Then was not non-existent nor existent: there was no realm of air, no sky beyond it.

   What covered in, and where? and what gave shelter? Was water there, unfathomed depth of water?

2. Death was not then, nor was there aught immortal: no sign was there, the day's and night's divider.

   That One Thing, breathless, breathed by its own nature: apart from it was nothing whatsoever.

3. Darkness there was: at first concealed in darkness this All was in discriminated chaos.

   All that existed then was void and formless: by the great power of Warmth was born that Unit.

4. Thereafter rose Desire in the beginning, Desire, the primal seed and germ of Spirit.

   Sages who searched with their heart's thought discovered the existent's kinship in the non-existent.

5. Transversely was their severing line extended: what was above it then, and what below it?

   There were begetters, there were nightly forces, free action here and energy up yonder.

6. Who verily knows and who can here declare it, whence it was born and whence comes this creation?

   The Gods are later than this world's Production. Who knows then whence it first came into being?

7. He, the first origin of this creation, whether he formed it all or did not form it,

   Whose eye controls this world in highest heaven, he verily knows it, or perhaps he knows not.

(X/129)

•

Madhuchchhanda

1. From Fervour kindled to its height Eternal Law and Truth were born:

Thence was the Night produced, and thence the billowy flood of sea arose.

2. From that same billowy flood of sea the Year was afterwards produced,

   Ordainer of the days and nights, Lord over all who close the eye.

3. Dhatar, the great Creator, then formed in due order Sun and Moon.

   He formed in order Heaven and Earth, the regions of the air, and light.

(X/190)

PURUSA: THE UNIVERSAL SOUL

Narayana

Purusa, embodied spirit, or Man personified and regarded as the soul and original source of the universe, the personal and life-giving principle in all animated beings, is said to have a thousand, that is, innumerable, heads, eyes, and feet, as being one with all created life. A space ten fingers wide: the region of the heart of man, wherein the soul was supposed to reside. Although as the Universal Soul he pervades the universe, as the Individual Soul he is enclosed in a space of narrow dimensions.

1. A thousand heads hath Purusa, a thousand eyes, a thousand feet.

   On every side pervading earth he fills a space ten fingers wide.

2. This Purusa is all that yet hath been and all that is to be;

   The Lord of Immortality which waxes greater still by food.

3. So mighty is his greatness; yea, greater than this is Purusa.

All creatures are one-fourth of him, three fourths eternal life in heaven.

4. With three-fourths Purusa went up: one-fourth of him again was here.

   Thence he strod out to every side over what eats not and what eats.

5. From him Viraj was born; again Purusa from Viraj was born.

   As soon as he was born he spread eastward and westward o'er the earth.

6. When Gods prepared the sacrifice with Purusa as their offering,

   Its oil was spring, the holy gift was autumn; summer was the wood.

7. They balmed as victim on the grass Purusa born in earliest time.

   With him the Deities and all Sadhyas and Rishis sacrificed.

8. From that great general sacrifice the dripping fat was gathered up.

   He formed the creatures of the air, and animals both wild and tame.

9. From that great general sacrifice Richas and Sama-hymns were born:

   Therefrom were spells and charms produced; the Yajus had its birth from it.

10. From it were horses born, from it all cattle with two rows of teeth:

    From it were generated kine, from it the goats and sheep were born.

11. When they divided Purusa how many portions did they make?

What do they call his mouth, his arms? What do they call his thighs and feet?

12. The Brahmin was his mouth, of both his arms was the Rajanya made.

    His thighs became the Vaishya, from his feet the Shudra was produced.

13. The Moon was gendered from his mind, and from his eye the Sun had birth;

    Indra and Agni from his mouth were born, and Vayu from his breath.

14. Forth from his navel came mid-air; the sky was fashioned from his head;

    Earth from his feet, and from his ear the regions. Thus they formed the worlds.

15. Seven fencing-sticks had he, thrice seven layers of fuel were prepared,

    When the Gods, offering sacrifice, bound, as their victim, Purusa.

16. Gods, sacrificing, sacrificed the victim: these were the earliest holy ordinances.

    The Mighty Ones attained the height of heaven, there were the Sadhyas, Gods of old, are dwelling.

(X/90)

MAYABHEDA: ILLUSION

Prajapati

The subject is Mayabheda, the discernment of maya, or illusion, the cause of material creation.

1. The sapient with their spirit and their mind behold the Bird adorned with all an Asura's magic might.

   Sages observe him in the ocean's inmost depth: the wise disposers seek the station of his rays.

2. The flying Bird bears Speech within his spirit: erst the Gandharva in the womb pronounced it:

   And at the seat of sacrifice the sages cherish this radiant heavenly-bright invention.

3. I saw the Herdsman, him who never resteth, approaching and departing on his pathways.

   He, clothed in gathered and diffusive splendour, within the worlds continually travels.

(X/177)

DYAVA-PRITHIVI: HEAVEN AND EARTH

Auchathya

1. These, Heaven and Earth, bestow prosperity on all, sustainers of the region, Holy Ones and wise,

   Two Bowls of noble kind: between these Goddesses the God, the fulgent Sun, travels by fixed decree.

2. Widely-capacious Pair, mighty, that never fail, the Father and the Mother keep all creatures safe:

   The two world-halves, the spirited, the beautiful, because the Father hath clothed them in goodly forms.

3. Son of these Parents, he the Priest with power to cleanse, Sage, sanctifies the worlds with his surpassing power.

   Thereto for his bright milk he milked through all the days the party-coloured Cow and the prolific Bull.

4. Among the skilful Gods most skilled is he, who made the two world-halves which bring prosperity to all;

Who with great wisdom measured both the regions out, and established them with pillars that shall ne'er decay.

5. Extolled in song, O Heaven and Earth, bestow on us, ye mighty Pair, great glory and high lordly sway,

   Whereby we may extend ourselves ever over the folk; and send us strength that shall deserve the praise of men.

(I/160)

•

Agastya

1. Whether of these is older, whether later? How were they born? Who knoweth it, ye sages?

   These of themselves support all things existing: as on a car the Day and Night roll onward.

2. The Twain uphold, though motionless and footless, a widespread offspring having feet and moving.

   Like your own son upon his parents' bosom, protect us, Heaven and Earth, from fearful danger.

3. I call for Aditi's unrivalled bounty, perfect, celestial, deathless, meet for worship.

   Produce this, ye Twain Worlds, for him who lauds you. Protect us, Heaven and Earth, from fearful danger.

4. May we be close to both the Worlds who suffer no pain, Parents of Gods, who aid with favour,

   Both mid the gods, with Day and Night alternate. Protect us, Heaven and Earth, from fearful danger.

5. Faring together, young, with meeting limits, Twin Sisters lying in their Parents' bosom,

Kissing the centre of the world together. Protect us, Heaven and Earth, from fearful danger.

6. Duly I call the two wide seats, the mighty, the general Parents, with the God's protection.

Who, beautiful to look on, make the nectar. Protect us, Heaven and Earth, from fearful danger.

7. Wide, vast, and manifold, whose bounds are distant, —these, reverent, I address at this our worship,

The blessed Pair, victorious, all-sustaining. Protect us, Heaven and Earth, from fearful danger.

8. What sin we have at any time committed against the Gods, our friend, our house's chieftain,

Thereof may this our hymn be expiation. Protect us, Heaven and Earth, from fearful danger.

9. May both these Friends of man, who bless, preserve me, may they attend me with their help and favour.

Enrich the man more liberal than the godless. May we, ye Gods, be strong with food rejoicing.

10. Endowed with understanding, I have uttered this truth, for all to hear, to Earth and Heaven.

Be near us, keep us from reproach and trouble. Father and Mother, with your help preserve us.

11. Be this my prayer fulfilled, O Earth and Heaven, wherewith, Father and Mother I address you.

Nearest of Gods be ye with your protection. May we find strengthening food in full abundance.

(I/185)

PRITHIVI: EARTH

Atri

1. Thou, of a truth, O' Prithivi, bearest the tool that rends the hills:

   Thou rich in torrents, who with might quickens earth, O Mighty One.

2. To thee, O wanderer at will, ring out the lauds with beams of day,

   Who drivest, like a neighing steed, the swelling cloud, O bright of hue.

3. Who graspest with thy might on earth e'en the strong sovrans of the wood,

   When from the lightning of thy cloud the rainfloods of the heaven descend.

(V/84)

AAPAH: WATERS

Vasishtha

1. Forth from the middle of the flood the Waters—their chief the Sea—flow cleansing, never sleeping.

   Indra, the Bull, the Thunderer, dug their channels: here let those Waters, Goddesses, protect me.

2. Waters which come from heaven, or those that wander dug from the earth, or flowing free by nature,

   Bright, purifying, speeding to the Ocean, here let those Waters, Goddesses, protect me.

3. Those amid whom goes Varuna the Sovran, he who discriminates men's truth and falsehood

   Distilling meath, the bright, the purifying, here let those Waters, Goddesses, protect me.

4. They from whom Varuna the King, and Soma, and all the Deities drink strength and vigour,

They into whom Vaishvanara Agni entered, here let those Waters, Goddesses, protect me.

(VII/49)

Manas: Spirit

Bandhu

The Hymn is an address to recall the fleeting spirit of a man at the point of death.

1. Thy spirit, that went far away to Yama, Vivasvan's Son,

   We cause to come to thee again that thou mayst live and sojourn here.

2. Thy spirit, that went far away, that passed away to earth and heaven,

   We cause to come to thee again that thou Mayst live and sojourn here.

3. Thy spirit, that went far away, away to the four-cornered earth,

   We cause to come to thee again that thou mayst live and sojourn here.

4. Thy spirit, that went far away to the four quarters of the world,

   We cause to come to thee again that thou mayst live and sojourn here.

5. Thy spirit, that went far away, away unto the billowy sea,

   We cause to come to thee again that thou mayst live and sojourn here.

6. Thy Spirit, that went far away to beams of light that Flash and Flow,

We cause to come to thee again that thou mayst live and sojourn here.

7. Thy spirit, that went far away, went to the waters and the plants,

   We cause to come to thee again that thou mayst live and sojourn here.

8. Thy spirit, that went far away, that visited the Sun and Dawn,

   We cause to come to thee again that thou mayst live and sojourn here.

9. Thy spirit, that went far away, away to lofty mountain heights,

   We cause to come to thee again that thou mayst live and sojourn here.

10. Thy spirit, that went far away into this All that lives and moves,

    We cause to come to thee again that thou mayst live and sojourn here.

11. Thy spirit, that went far away to distant realms beyond our ken,

    We cause to come to thee again that thou mayst live and sojourn here.

12. Thy spirit, that went far away to all that is and is to be,

    We cause to come to thee again that thou mayst live and sojourn here.

(X/58)

VAK: SPEECH

Vagambhrani

Vak is Speech personified, the Word, the first creation and representative of Spirit, and the means of communication between men and Gods. The hymn shows

that the primary application of the name was to the voice of the hymn, the means of communication between heaven and earth at the sacrifice.

1. I travel with the Rudras and the Vasus, with the Adityas and All-Gods I wander.

   I hold aloft both Varuna and Mitra, Indra and AgnL and the Pair of Asvins.

2. I cherish and sustain high-swelling Soma, and Tvastar I support, Pusan, and Bhaga.

   I load with wealth the zealous sacrificer who pours the juice and offers his oblation.

3. I am the Queen, the gatherer-up of treasures, most thoughtful, first of those who merit worship.

   Thus Gods have established me in many places with many homes to enter and abide in.

4. Through me alone all eat the food that feeds them—each man who sees, breathes, hears the word outspoken.

   They know it not, but yet they dwell beside me. Hear, one and all, the truth as I declare it.

5. I, verily, myself announce and utter the word that Gods and men alike shall welcome.

   I make the man I love exceeding mighty, make him a sage, a Rishi, and a Brahmin.

6. I bend the bow for Rudra that his arrow may strike and slay the hater of devotion.

   I rouse and order, battle for the people, and I have penetrated Earth and Heaven.

7. On the world's summit I bring forth the Father: my home is in the waters, in the ocean.

Thence I extend o'er all existing creatures, and touch even yonder heaven with my forehead.

8. I breathe a strong breath like wind and tempest, the while I hold together all existence.

   Beyond this wide earth and beyond the heavens I have become so mighty in my grandeur.

(X/125)

SHRADDHA: FAITH

Kamayani

1. By Faith is Agni kindled, through Faith is oblation offered up.

   We celebrate with praises Faith upon the height of happiness.

2. Bless thou the man who gives, O Faith; Faith, bless the man who fain would give.

   Bless thou the liberal worshippers: bless thou the word that I have said.

3. Even as the Deities maintained Faith in the mighty Asuras,

   So make this uttered wish of mine true for the liberal worshippers.

4. Guarded by Vayu, Gods and men who sacrifice to draw near to Faith.

   Man winneth Faith by yearnings of the heart and opulence by Faith.

5. Faith in the early morning, Faith at noon-day will we invocate,

   Faith at the setting of the Sun. O Faith, endow us with belief.

(X/151)

Jnana: Knowledge

Brihaspati

Jnana or Knowledge, the subject of this very difficult hymn, is said by Sayana to mean Parama-brahmajnanam, knowledge of the higher truths of Religion, which teaches man his own nature and how he may be reunited to the Supreme Spirit.

1. When men, Brihaspati, giving names to objects, sent out Vak's first and earliest utterances,

   All that was excellent and spotless, treasured within them, was disclosed through their affection.

2. Where, like men cleansing corn flour in a cribble, the wise in spirit have created language,

   Friends see and recognize the marks of friendship: their speech retains the blessed sign imprinted.

3. With sacrifice the trace of Vak they followed, and found her harbouring within the Rishis.

   They brought her, dealt her forth in many places: seven singers make her tones resound in concert.

4. One man hath ne'er seen Vak, and yet he seeth: One man hath hearing but hath never heard her.

   But to another hath she shown her beauty as a fond well-dressed woman to her husband.

5. One man they call a laggard, dull in friendship: they never urge him on to deeds of valour.

   He wanders on in profitless illusion: the Voice he heard yields neither fruit nor blossom.

6. No part in Vak hath he who hath abandoned his own dear friend who knows the truth of friendship.

   Even if he hears her still in vain he listens: naught knows he of the path of righteous action.

7. Unequal in the quickness of their spirit are friends endowed alike with eyes and hearing,

   Some look like tanks that reach the mouth or shoulder, others like pools of water fit to bathe in.

8. When friendly Brahmins sacrifice together with mental impulse which the heart hath fashioned,

   They leave one far behind through their attainments, and some who count as Brahmins wander elsewhere.

9. Those men who step not back and move not forward, nor Brahmins nor preparers of libations,

   Having attained to Vak in sinful fashion spin out their thread in ignorance like spinsters.

10. All friends are joyful in the friend who cometh in triumph, having conquered in assembly.

    He is their blame-averter, food-provider: prepared is he and fit for deeds of vigour.

11. One plies his constant task reciting verses: one sings the holy psalm in Shakvari measures.

    One more, the Brahmin, tells the lore of being, and one lays down the rules of sacrificing.

(X/71)

Agni: God of Fire

Madhucchandas

The first hymn of the Rigveda is ascribed to the Rishi or seer Madhucchandas Vaisvamitra, a son or descendant of the famous Visvamitra. The deity to whom this hymn is addressed is Agni, the God of fire, the most prominent of the deities of the Rigveda. Agni is the messenger and mediator between earth and heaven, announcing to the Gods the hymns, and conveying to them the oblations of their worshippers, inviting them with the sound of his crackling flames and bringing them down to the place of sacrifice.

1. I laud Agni, the chosen Priest, God, minister of sacrifice,

   The hotar, lavishest of wealth.

2. Worthy is Agni to be praised by living as by ancient seers.

   He shall bring hitherward the Gods.

3. Through Agni man obtains wealth, yea, plenty waxing day by day.

   Most rich in heroes, glorious.

4. Agni, the perfect sacrifice which thou encompassest about

   Verily goeth to the Gods.

5. May Agni, sapient-minded Priest. truthfuL most gloriously great,

   The God, come hither with the Gods.

6. Whatever blessing, Agni, thou wilt grant unto thy worshipper,

   That, Angiras, is indeed thy truth.

7. To thee, dispeller of the night, O Agni, day by day with prayer

   Bringing thee reverence, we come;

8. Ruler of sacrifices, guard of Law eternal, radiant One,

   Increasing in thine own abode.

9. Be to us easy of approach, even as a father to his son:

   Agni, be with us for our weal.

(I/1)

•

—Bharadwaja

1. With this my song I strive to reach this guest of yours, who wakes at early morn, the Lord of all the tribes.

   Each time he comes from heaven, the Pure One from of old: from ancient days the Child eats everlasting food.

2. Whom, well-disposed, the Bhrigus established as a Friend, whom men must glorify, high-flaming in the wood.

   As such, most friendly, thou art every day extolled in lauds by Vitahavya, O thou wondrous God.

3. Be thou the foeless helper of the skilful man, subduer of the enemy near or far away.

   Bestow a wealthy home on men, O Son of Strength. Give Vitahavya riches spreading far and wide, give Bharadwaja widespread wealth.

4. Him, your refulgent guest, Agni who comes from heaven, the Herald of mankind, well-skilled in sacred rites,

   Who, like a holy singer, utters heavenly words, oblation-bearer, envoy, God, I seek with hymns.

5. Who with his purifying, eye-attracting form hath shone upon the earth as with the light of Dawn;

   Who speeding on, as in the fight of Etasa, cometh, untouched by age, as one athirst in heat.

6. Worship ye AgnL with your log of wood; praise your beloved, your beloved guest with songs.

   Invite ye the Immortal hither with your hymns. A God among the Gods, he loveth what is choice, loveth our service, God mid Gods.

7. Agni inflamed with fuel in my song I sing, pure, cleanser, steadfast, set in front at sacrifice.

Wise Jatavedas we implore with prayers for bliss the Priest, the holy Singer, bounteous, void of guile.

8. Men, Agni, in each age have made thee, Deathless One, their envoy, offering-bearer, guard adorable.

With reverence Gods and mortals have established thee, the ever-watchfuL omnipresent Household Lord.

9. Thou, AgnL ordering the works and ways of both, as envoy of the Gods traverse both the worlds.

When we lay claim to thy regard and gracious care, be thou to us a thrice protecting friendly guard.

10. Him fair of face, rapid, and fair to look on, him very wise may we who know not follow.

Let him who knows all rules invite for worship, Agni announce our offering to the Immortals.

11. Him, AgnL thou delivers and saves who brings him prayer to thee the Wise, 0 Hero,

The end of sacrifice or its inception; yea, thou endowest him with power and riches.

12. Guard us from him who would assail us. Agni; preserve us, 0 thou Victor, from dishonour.

Here let the place of darkening come upon thee: may wealth be ours, desirable in thousands.

13. Agni, the Priest, is King, Lord of the homestead, he, Jatavedas, knows all generations.

Most skilful worshipper mid Gods and mortals, may he begin the sacrifice, the Holy.

14. Whate'er to-day thou, bright-flamed Priest, enjoyest from the man's rite — for thou art sacrificer—

Worship, for duly dost thou spread in greatness: bear off thine offerings of today, Most Youthful.

15. Look thou upon the viands duly laid for thee. Fain would he set thee here to worship Heaven and Earth.

Help us, O liberal AgnL in the strife for spoiL so that we may o'ercome all things that trouble, o'ercome them with thy help.

16. Together with all Gods, 0 fair-faced AgnL be seated first upon the wool-lined altar,

Nest-like, bedewed with oil. Bear this our worship to Savitar who sacrifices rightly.

17. Here the arranging priests, as did Atharvan, rub this Agni forth,

Whom, not bewildered, as he moved in winding ways, they brought from gloom.

18. For the Gods' banquet be thou born, for full perfection and for weal,

Bring the Immortal Gods who strengthen holy Law: so let our sacrifice reach the Gods.

19. O Agni, Lord and Master of men's homesteads, with kindled fuel we have made thee mighty.

Let not our household gear be found defective. Sharpen us with thy penetrating splendour.

(VI/15)

Indra: Warrior God

Madhuchchandas

Indra was the favourite national deity of the Aryans, in the Vedic Age, and more hymns are dedicated to his honour than to the praise of any other divinity. He is the God who reigns over the intermediate region or atmosphere; he fights against and conquers with his thunderbolt the demons of draughts and darkness, and is in general the type of noble heroism.

1. As a good cow to him who milks, we call the doer of fair deeds,

   To our assistance day by day.

2. Come thou to our libations, drink of Soma, Soma-drinker thou!

   The rich One's rapture giveth kine.

3. So may we be acquainted with thine innermost benevolence:

   Neglect us not, come hitherward.

4. Go to the wise unconquered One, ask thou of Indra, skilled in song,

   Him who is better than thy friends.

5. Whether the men who mock us say, Depart unto another place,

   Ye who serve Indra and none else;

6. Or whether, God of wondrous deeds, all our true people call us blest,

   Still may we dwell in Indra's care.

7. Unto the swift One bring the swift, man-cheering, grace of sacrifice,

   That to the Friend gives wings and joy.

8. Thou, Shatakratu, drankest this and wast the Vritras' slayer; thou

   Helpest the warrior in the fray.

9. We strengthen, Shatakratu, thee, yea, thee the powerful in fight,

   That, Indra, we may win us wealth.

10. To him the mighty stream of wealth, prompt friend of him who pours the juice,

    Yea, to this Indra sing your song.

(I/4)

Soma: Energy Drink

Vishwamitra

Soma is the God who represents and animates the juice of the Soma plant. He was in former times the Indian Dionysus or Bacchus. 'The simple-minded Aryan people,' says Professor Whitney, 'whose whole religion was a worship of the wonderful powers and phenomena of nature, had no sooner perceived that Soma juice had power to elevate the spirits, and produce a temporary frenzy, under the influence of which the individual was prompted to and capable of, deeds beyond his natural powers, than they found in it something divine: it was to their apprehension a God, endowing those into whom it entered with godlike powers; the plant which afforded it became to them the king of plants; the process of preparing it became a holy sacrifice.

1. In sweetest and most gladdening stream flow pure, O Soma, on thy way,

   Pressed out for Indra, for his drink.
2. Fiend-queller, Friend of all men, he hath with the wood attained unto

   His place, his iron-fashioned home.
3. Be thou best Vritra-slayer, best granter of bliss, most liberal:

   Promote our wealthy princes' gifts.
4. Flow onward with thy juice unto the banquet of the Mighty Gods:

   Flow hither for our strength and fame.

5. O Indu, we draw nigh to thee, with this one object day by day:

   To thee alone our prayers are said.

6. By means of this eternal fleece may Surya's Daughter purify

   Thy Soma that is foaming forth.

7. Ten sister maids of slender form seize him within the press and hold

   Him firmly on the final day.

8. The virgins send him forth: they blow the skin musician-like and fuse

   The triple foe-repelling meath.

9. Inviolable milch-kine round about him blend for Indra's drink,

   The fresh young Soma with their milk.

10. In the wild raptures of this draught, Indra slays all the Vritras: he,

    The Hero, pours his wealth on us.

(IX/1)

MITRA: LIGHT-GOD

Vishwamitra

1. Mitra, when speaking, stirreth men to labour: Mitra sustaineth both the earth and heaven.

   Mitra beholdeth men with eyes that close not. To Mitra bring, with holy oil, oblation.

2. Foremost be he who brings thee food, O Mitra, who strives to keep thy sacred Law, Aditya.

   He whom thou helpest ne'er is slain or conquered, on him, from near or far, falls no affliction.

3. Joying in sacred food and freed from sickness, with knees bent lowly on the earth's broad surface,

Following closely the Aditya's statute, may we remain in Mitra's gracious favour.

4. Auspicious and adorable, this Mitra was born with fair dominion, King, Disposer.

   May we enjoy the grace of him the Holy, yea, rest in his propitious loving-kindness.

5. The great Aditya, to be served with worship, who stirreth men, is gracious to the singer.

   To Mitra, him most highly to be lauded, offer in fire oblation that he loveth.

6. The gainful grace of Mitra, God, supporter of the race of man,

   Gives splendour of most glorious fame.

7. Mitra whose glory spreads afar, he who in might surpasses heaven,

   Surpasses earth in his renown.

8. All the Five Races have repaired to Mitra, ever strong to aid.

   For he sustaineth all the Gods.

9. Mitra to Gods, to living men, to him who strews the holy grass,

   Gives food fulfilling sacred Law.

(III/59)

Varuna: God of Moral Order

Ajigarta

Varuna is the chief of the lords of natural order. His activity displays itself pre-eminently in the control of the most regular phenomena of nature. Varuna is King of the air and of the sea, the latter being often regarded as identical with the former.

1. Whatever law of thine, O God, O Varuna, as we are men,

   Day after day we violate.

2. Give us not as a prey to death, to be destroyed by thee in wrath,

   To thy fierce anger when displeased.

3. To gain thy mercy, Varuna, with hymns we bind thy heart, as binds

   The charioteer his tethered horse.

4. They flee from me dispirited, bent only on obtaining wealth,

   As to their nests the birds of air.

5. When shall we bring, to be appeased, the Hero, Lord of warrior might,

   Him, the far-seeing Varuna?

6. This, this with joy the both accept in common: never do they fail

   The ever-faithful worshipper.

7. He knows the path of birds that fly through heaven, and, Sovran of the sea,

   He knows the ships that are thereon.

8. True to his holy law, he knows the twelve moons with their progeny:

   He knows the moon of later birth.

9. He knows the pathway of the wind, the spreading, high, and mighty wind:

   He knows the Gods who dwell above.

10. Varuna, true to holy law, sits down among his people; he,

    Most wise, sits there to govern all.

11. From thence perceiving he beholds all things, both what hath been,

    And what hereafter will be done.

12. May that Aditya, very wise, make fair paths for us all our days:

    May he prolong our lives for us.

13. Varuna, wearing golden mail, hath clad him in a shining robe:

    His spies are seated round about.

14. The God whom enemies threaten not, nor those who tyrannize o'er men,

    Nor those whose minds are bent on wrong.

15. He who gives glory to mankind, not glory that is incomplete,

    To our own bodies giving it.

16. Yearning for the wide-seeing One, my thoughts move onward unto him,

    As kine unto their pastures move.

17. Once more together let us speak, because my meath is brought: priest-like

    Thou feastest what is dear to thee.

18. Now saw I him whom all may see, I saw his car above the earth:

    He hath accepted these my songs.

19. Varuna, hear this call of mine: be gracious unto us this day

    Longing for help I cried to thee.

20. Thou, O wise God, art Lord of all, thou art the King of earth and heaven:

    Hear, as thou goest on thy way.

21. Release us from the upper bond, untie the bond between, and loose

    The bonds below, that I may live.

(I/25)

Ashvins: Two Horsemen

Praskanva

The Ashvins seem to have been a puzzle even to the oldest Indian commentators. Yaska asks: 'Who are these Ashvins?' 'Heaven and Earth', say some. Day and Night, Sun and Moon, or Two kings, say others. Roth says, 'The two Ashvins hold a distinct position in the entire body of the deities of light. They are the earliest bringers of light in the morning sky, who in their chariots hasten onward before the dawn, and prepare the way for.'

1. Now Morning with her earliest light shines forth, dear Daughter of the Sky:

    High, Ashvins, I extol your praise,

2. Sons of the Sea, mighty to save discoverers of riches, ye

    Gods with deep thought who find out wealth.

3. Your giant coursers hasten on over the region all in flames,

    When your car flies with winged steeds.

4. He, liberal, lover of the flood, Lord of the House, the vigilant,

    Chiefs! with oblations feeds you full.

5. Ye have regard unto our hymns, Nasatyas, thinking of our words:

    Drink boldly of the Soma juice.

6. Vouchsafe to us, O Ashvin Pair, such strength as, with attendant light,

   May through the darkness carry us.

7. Come in the ship of these our hymns to bear you to the hither shore:

   O Ashvins, harness ye the car.

8. The heaven's wide vessel is your own: on the flood's shore your chariot waits:

   Drops, with the hymn, have been prepared.

9. Kanvas, the drops are in the heaven; the wealth is at the waters' place:

   Where will ye manifest your form?

10. Light came to lighten up the branch, the Sun appeared as it were gold:

    And with its tongue shone forth the dark.

11. The path of sacrifice was made to travel to the farther goal:

    The road of heaven was manifest.

12. The singer of their praise awaits whatever grace the Ashvins give,

    Who save when Soma gladdens them.

13. Ye dwellers with Vivasvan come, auspicious, as to Manu erst;

    Come to the Soma and our praise.

14. O circumambient Ashvins, Dawn follows the brightness of your way:

    Approve with beams our solemn rites.

15. Drink ye of our libations, grant protection, O ye Ashvins Twain,

    With aids which none may interrupt.

(I/46)

Vayu: God of Wind

Vamadeva

1. Taste offerings never tasted yet, as bards enjoy the foeman's wealth.

   O Vayu, on refulgent car come to the drinking of the juice.

2. Removing curses, drawn by teams, with Indra seated by thy side,

   O Vayu, on refulgent car come to the drinking of the juice.

3. The two dark treasuries of wealth that wear all beauties wait on thee,

   O Vayu, on refulgent car come to the drinking of the juice.

4. May nine-and-ninety harnessed steeds who yoke them at thy will bring thee.

   O Vayu, on refulgent car come to the drinking of the juice.

5. Harness, O Vayu, to thy car a hundred well-fed tawny steeds,

   Yea, or a thousand steeds, and let thy chariot come to us with might.

(IV /48)

Rudra: Tempest God

Kutsa

Rudra: generally explained as the Roarer, from the sound is stormy winds, the God of tempests and father of the Maruts. He is called Kapardin as wearing hair braided and knotted like a cowry shell (kaparda) *derives Rudra (the Red, the Brilliant) from a lost root rud, to be red.*

1. To the strong Rudra bring we these our songs of praise, to him the Lord of Heroes, with the braided hair,

   That it be well with all our cattle and our men, that in this village all be healthy and well-fed.

2. Be gracious unto us, O Rudra, bring us joy: thee, Lord of Heroes, thee with reverence will we serve.

   Whatever health and strength our father Manu won by sacrifice may we, under thy guidance, gain.

3. By worship of the Gods may we, O Bounteous One, O Rudra, gain thy grace, Ruler of valiant men.

   Come to our families, bringing them bliss: may we, whose heroes are uninjured, bring thee sacred gifts,

4. Hither we call for aid the wise, the wanderer, impetuous Rudra, perfecter of sacrifice.

   May he repel from us the anger of the Gods: verily, we desire his favourable grace.

5. Him with the braided hair we call with reverence down, the wild-boar of the sky, the red, the dazzling shape.

   May he, his hand filled full of sovran medicines, grant us protection, shelter, and a home secure.

6. To him the Maruts' Father is this hymn addressed, to strengthen Rudra's might a song more sweet than sweet.

   Grant us, Immortal One, the food which mortals eat: be gracious unto me, my seed, my progeny,

7. O Rudra, harm not either great or small of us, harm not the growing boy, harm not the full-grown man,

Slay not a sire among us, slay no mother here, and to our own dear bodies, Rudra, do not harm.

8. Harm us not Rudra, in our seed and progeny, harm us not in the living, nor in cows or steeds,

   Slay not our heroes in the fury of thy wrath, Bringing oblations evermore we call to thee.

9. Even as a herdsman I have brought thee hymns of praise: O Father of the Maruts, give us happiness.

   Blessed is thy most favouring benevolence, so, verily, do we desire thy saving help.

10. Far be thy dart that killeth men or cattle: thy bliss be with us, O thou Lord of Heroes.

    Be gracious unto us, O God, and bless us, and then vouchsafe us doubly-strong protection.

11. We, seeking help, have spoken and adored him: may Rudra, girt by Maruts, hear our calling.

    This prayer of ours may Varuna grant and Mitra, and Aditi and Sindhu, Earth and Heaven.

(I/114)

Visnu: The Pervader of All

Auchathya

This God, 'the all-pervading or encompassing,' is not placed in the Veda in the foremost rank of deities, and, though frequently invoked with Indra, Varuna, the Maruts, Rudra, Vayu and the Adityas, his superiority to them is never stated, and he is even described in one place as celebrating the praise of Indra and deriving his power from that God. The point which distinguishes him from the other Vedic deities is chiefly his striding over the heavens, which he is said to do in three paces.

1. I will declare the mighty deeds of Visnu, of him who measured out the earthly regions,

Who propped the highest place of congregation, thrice setting down his footstep, widely striding.

2. For this his mighty deed is Visnu lauded, like some wild beast, dread, prowling, mountain-roaming;

He within whose three wide-extended paces all living creatures have their habitation.

3. Let the hymn lift itself as strength to Visnu, the Bull far-striding, dwelling on the mountains,

Him who alone with triple step hath measured this common dwelling-place, long, far extended.

4. Him whose three paces that are filled with sweetness, imperishable, joy as it may list them,

Who, verily, alone upholds the threefold, the earth, the heaven, and all living creatures.

5. May I attain to that his well-loved mansion where men devoted to the Gods are happy.

For there springs, close akin to the Wide-Strider, the well of meath in Visnu's highest footstep.

6. Fain would we go unto your dwelling places where there are many-horned and nimble oxen,

For mightily, there, shineth down upon us the widely-striding Bull's sublimest mansion.

(I/154)

Surya : The Sun

Praskanva

1. His bright rays bear him up aloft, the God who knoweth all that lives,

Surya, that all may look on him.

2. The constellations pass away, like thieves, together with their beams,

Before the all-beholding Sun.

3. His herald rays are seen afar refulgent o'er the world of men,

   Like flames of fire that burn and blaze.

4. Swift and all beautiful art thou, O Surya, maker of the light,

   Illumine all the radiant realm.

5. Thou goest to the hosts of Gods, thou comest hither to mankind,

   Hither all light to be beheld.

6. With that same eye of thine wherewith thou lookest, brilliant Varuna,

   Upon the busy race of men,

7. Traversing sky and wide mid-air, thou metest with thy beams our days,

   Sun, seeing all things that have birth.

8. Seven Bay Steeds harnessed to thy car bear thee, O thou farseeing One,

   God, Surya, with the radiant hair.

9. Surya hath yoked the pure bright Seven, the daughters of the car; with these,

   His own dear team, he goeth forth.

10. Looking upon the loftier light above the darkness we have come

    To Surya, God among the Gods, the light that is most excellent.

11. Rising this day, O rich in friends, ascending to the loftier heaven,

    Surya, remove my heart's disease, take from me this my yellow hue.

12. To parrots and to starlings let us give away my yellowness,

Or this my yellowness let us transfer to Haritala trees.

13. With all his conquering vigour this Aditya hath gone up on high,

    Giving my foe into mine hand: let me not be my foeman's prey.

(I/501)

Gavah : Cows

Bharadwaj

1. The Kine have come and brought good fortune: let them rest in the cow-pen and be happy near us.

   Here let them stay prolific, many-coloured, and yield through many morns their milk for Indra.

2. Indra aids him who offers sacrifice and gifts: he takes not what is his, and gives him more thereto.

   Increasing ever more and ever more his wealth, he makes the pious dwell within unbroken bounds.

3. These are ne'er lost, no robber ever injures them: no evil-minded foe attempts to harass them.

   The master of the Kine lives many a year with these, the cows whereby he pours his gifts and serves the Gods.

4. The charger with his dusty brow O'ertakes them not, and never to the shambles do they take their way.

   These Cows, the cattle of the pious worshipper, roam over widespread pasture where no danger is.

5. To me the Cows seem Bhaga, they seem Indra, they seem a portion of the first poured Soma,

   These present Cows, they, O ye men, are Indra. I long for Indra with my heart and spirit.

6. O Cows, ye fatten e'en the worn and wasted, and make the unlovely beautiful to look on.

   Prosper my house, ye with auspicious voices. Your power is glorified in our assemblies.

7. Crop goodly pasturage and be prolific: drink pure sweet water at good drinking places.

   Never be thief or sinful man your master, and may the dart of Rudra still avoid you.

8. Now let this close admixture be close intermigled with these Cows,

   Mixt with the Steer's prolific flow, and, Indra, with thy hero might.

(VI/281)

MANDUKAH: FROGS

Vasishtha

1. They who lay quiet for a year, the Brahmins who fulfil their vows,

   The Frogs have lifted up their voice, the voice parjanya hath inspired.

2. What time on these, as on a dry skin lying in the pool's bed, the floods of heaven descended,

   The music of the Frogs comes forth in concert like the cows lowing with their calves beside them.

3. When at the coming of the Rains the water has poured upon them as they yearned and thirsted,

   One seeks another as he talks and greets him with cries of pleasure as a son his father.

4. Each of these twain receives the other kindly, while they are revelling in the flow of waters,

When the Frog moistened by the rain springs forward, and Green and Spotty both combine their voices.

5. When one of these repeats the other's language, as he who learns the lesson of the teacher,

Your every limb seems to be growing larger as ye converse with eloquence on the waters.

6. One is Cow-bellow and Goat-bleat the other, one Frog is Green and one of them is Spotty.

They bear one common name, and yet they vary, and, talking, modulate the voice diversely.

7. As Brahmins, sitting round the brimful vessel, talk at the Soma-rite of Atiratra,

So, Frogs, ye gather round the pool to honour this day of all the year, the first of Rain-time.

8. These Brahmins with the Soma juice, performing their year-long rite, have lifted up their voices;

And these Adhvaryus, sweating with their kettles, come forth and show themselves, and none are hidden.

9. They keep the twelve month's God-appointed order, and never do the men neglect the season.

Soon as the Rain-time in the year returneth, these who were heated kettles gain their freedom.

10. Cow-bellow and Goat-bleat have granted riches, and Green and Spotty have vouchsafed us treasure.

The Frogs who give us cows in hundreds lengthen our lives in this most fertilizing season.

(VIII/103)

ANNAM: FOOD

Atri

1. Now will I glorify Food that upholds great strength,
   By whose invigorating power Trita rent Vritra limb from limb.
2. O pleasant Food, O Food of meath, thee have we chosen for our own,
   So be our kind protector thou.
3. Come hitherward to us, O Food, auspicious with auspicious help,
   Health-bringing, not unkind, a dear and guileless friend.
4. These juices which, O Food, are thine throughout the regions are diffused.
   Like winds they have their place in heaven.
5. These gifts of thine, O Food, O Food most sweet to taste,
   These savours of thy juices work like creatures that have mighty necks.
6. In thee, O Food, is set the spirit of great Gods.
   Under thy flag brave deeds were done: he slew the Dragon with thy help.
7. If thou be gone unto the splendour of the clouds,
   Even from thence, O Food of meath, prepared for our enjoyment, come.
8. Whatever morsel we consume from waters or from plants of earth,
   O Soma, wax thou fat thereby.
9. What, Soma, we enjoy from thee in milky food or barley-brew,
   Vatapi, grow thou fat thereby.

10. O Vegetable, Cake of meal, be wholesome, firm, and strengthening:

    Vatapi, grow thou fat thereby.

11. O Food, from thee as such have we drawn forth with lauds, like cows, our sacrificial gifts,

    From thee who banquetest with Gods, from thee who banquetest with us.

(I/187)

BRANCHES:
Some Upanishads

Isha Upanishad
God Pervades Everything

This short but valuable Upanishad provides excellent glimpses into the basic ideas of the Vedanta philosophy. It describes the nature and characteristics of Atman, the ethical conduct of one who knows it as well as a view of the beyond. Its unequivocal declaration that the Lord pervades the whole universe and allied beings, one should not covet others' goods and try to live within one's means and help the needy, may be taken as a commandment to human beings.

All this, whatsoever moves on earth, is to be hidden in the Lord. When thou hast surrendered all this, then thou mayest enjoy. Do not covet the wealth of any man!

Though a man may wish to live a hundred years, performing works, it will be thus with him; but not in any other way: work will thus not cling to a man.

There are the worlds of the Asuras covered with blind darkness. Those who have destroyed their self (who perform works, without having arrived at a knowledge of the true Self), go after death to those worlds.

That one, the Self, though never stirring, is swifter than thought. The Devas (senses) never reached it, it walked before them. Though standing still, it overtakes the others who are running. Matarishvan 'the wind, the moving spirit' bestows powers on it.

It strirs and it stirs not; it is far, and likewise near. It is inside of all this, and it is outside of all this.

And he who beholds all beings in the Self, and the Self in all beings, he never turns away from it.

When to a man who understands, the Self has become all things, what sorrow, what trouble can there be to him who once beheld that unity?

He 'the Self' encircled all, bright, incorporeal, scathless, without muscles, pure, untouched by evil; a seer, wise, omnipresent, self-existent, he disposed all things rightly for eternal years.

All who worship what is not real knowledge (good works), enter into blind darkness: those who delight in real knowledge, enter, as it were, into greater darkness.

One thing, they say, is obtained from real knowledge; another, they say, from what is not knowledge. Thus we have heard from the wise who taught us this.

He who knows at the same time both knowledge and not-knowledge, overcomes death through not-knowledge, and obtains immortality through knowledge.

All who worship what is not the true cause, enter into blind darkness: those who delight in the true cause, enter, as it were, into greater darkness.

One thing, they say, is obtained from knowledge of the cause; another, they say, from knowledge of what is not the cause. Thus we have heard from the wise who taught us this.

He who knows at the same time both the cause and the destruction (the perishable body), overcomes death by destruction (the perishable body), and obtains immortality through knowledge of the true cause.

The door of the True is covered with a golden disk.

Open that, O Pushan, that we may see the nature of the True.

O Pushan, only seer, Yama (Judge), Surya (sun), son of Prajapati, spread thy rays and gather them! The light which is thy fairest form, I see it. I am what He is, the person in the sun.

Breath to air, and to the immortal! Then this my body ends in ashes. Om! Mind, remember! Remember thy deeds! Mind, remember! Remember thy deeds!

Agni, lead us on to beatitude by a good path, thou, O God, who knowest all things! Keep far from us crooked evil, and we shall offer thee the fullest praise!

Kena Upanishad

Who gave us eyes, ears and speech . . .

*Who—*Kena*—gave us speech, makes us see and hear-are the questions answered in this short and beautiful Upanishad. Divided into two parts, the first in verse and the second in prose, it discusses the worship of Brahman, the Supreme power, with and without attributes. The concept of Brahman is India's contribution to philosophy, and its attainment the goal of human beings. The Upanishad provides insights into the subject.*

[1]

The Pupil asks: 'At whose wish does the mind sent forth proceed on its errand? At whose command does the first breath go forth? At whose wish do we utter this speech? What god directs the eye, or the ear?'

The Teacher replies: 'It is the ear of the ear, the mind of the mind, the speech of speech, the breath of breath, and the eye of the eye. When freed from the senses the wise, on departing from this world, become immortal.

'The eye does not go thither, nor speech, nor mind. We do not know, we do not understand, how anyone can teach it.

'It is different from the known, it is also above the unknown, thus we have heard from those of old, who taught us this.

'That which is not expressed by speech and by which speech is expressed, that alone know as Brahman, not that which people here adore.

'That which does not think by mind, and by which, they

say, mind is thought, that alone know as Brahman, not that which people here adore.

'That which does not see by the eye, and by which one sees the work of the eyes, that alone know as Brahman, not that which people here adore.

'That which does not hear by the ear, and by which the ear is heard, that alone know as Brahman, not that which people here adore.

'That which does not breathe by breath, and by which breath is drawn, that alone know as Brahman, not that which people here adore.'

(2)

The Teacher says: 'If thou thinkest I know it well, then thou knowest surely but little, what is that form of Brahman known, it may be, to thee?'

The Pupil says: 'I do not think I know it well, nor do I know that I do not know it. He among us who knows this, he knows it, nor does he know that he does not know it.

'He by whom the Brahman is not thought, by him it is thought; he by whom it is thought, knows it not. It is not understood by those who understand it, it is understood by those who do not understand it.

'It is thought to be known as if by awakening, and then we obtain immortality indeed. By the Self we obtain strength, by knowledge we obtain immortality.

'If a man know this here, that is the true end of life; if he does not know this here, then there is great destruction (new births). The wise who have thought on all things and recognised the Self in them become immortal, when they have departed from this world.'

(3)

Brahman obtained the victory for the Devas. The Devas became elated by the victory of Brahman, and they thought, this victory is ours only, this greatness is ours only.

Brahman perceived this and appeared to them. But they did not know it, and said: 'What sprite (Yaksha) is this?'

They said to Agni (fire): 'O Jatavedas, find out what sprite this is.' 'Yes,' he said.

He ran towards it, and Brahman said to him: 'Who are you?' He replied: 'I am Agni, I am Jatavedas.'

Brahman said: 'What power is in you?' Agni replied: 'I could burn all whatever there is on earth.'

Brahman put a straw before him, saying: 'Burn this.' He went towards it with all his might, but he could not bum it. Then he returned thence and said: 'I could not find out what sprite this is.'

Then they said to Vayu (air): 'O Vayu, find out what sprite this is.' 'Yes,' he said.

He ran towards it, and Brahman said to him: 'Who are you?' He replied: 'I am Vayu, I am Matarisvan.'

Brahman said: 'What power is in you?' Vayu replied: 'I could take up all whatever there is on earth.'

Brahman put a straw before him, saying: 'Take it up.' He went towards it with all his might, but he could not take it up. The he returned thence and said: 'I could not find out what sprite this is.'

Then they said to Indra: '0 Maghavan, find out what sprite this is.' He went towards it, but it disappeared from before him.

Then in the same space he came towards a woman, highly adorned: it was Uma, the daughter of Himavat. He said to her: 'Who is that sprite?'

She replied: 'It is Brahman. It is through the victory of Brahman that you have thus become great.' After that he knew that it was Brahman.

[4]

Therefore these Devas, Agni, Vayu, and Indra, are as it were, above the other gods, for they touched the Brahman nearest.

And therefore Indra is, as it were, above the other gods, for he touched it nearest, he first knew it.

This is the teaching of Brahman, with regard to the gods (mythological): It is that which now flashes forth in the lightning, and now vanishes again.

And this is the teaching of Brahman, with regard to the body (psychological): It is that which seems to move as mind, and by it imagination remembers again and again.

That Brahman is called Tadvana, by the name of Tadvana it is to be meditated on. All beings have a desire for him who knows this.

The Teacher: 'As you have asked me to tell you the Upanishad, the Upanishad has now been told you. We have told you the Brahma Upanishad.

'The feet on which that Upanishad stands are penance, restraint, sacrifice; the Vedas are all its limbs, the True is its abode.

'He who knows this Upanishad, and has shaken off all evil, stands in the endless, unconquerable world of heaven, yea, in the world of heaven.'

Katha Upanishad
'I shall go to death'

The Katha formed a school of the Black Yajurveda, which had developed five varieties of yajnas, or fire-ceremonies, one of which, the Nachiketas, was bestowed on him by Yama, the god of death, whom he pleased with his devotion. The Upanishad relates the interesting story as well as the ceremony, which ensures the attainment of an imperishable world which lies on the other side of the sun. It deals with the Atman as the subject of knowledge.

(1)

Vajashravasa, desirous of heavenly rewards, surrendered at a sacrifice all that he possessed. He had a son of the name of Nachiketas.

When the promised presents were being given to the priests, faith entered into the heart of Nachiketas, who was still a boy, and he thought:

'Unblessed, surely, are the worlds to which a man goes by giving as his promised present at a sacrifice cows which have drunk water, eaten hay, given their milk, and are barren.'

He knowing that his father had promised to give up all that he possessed, and therefore his son also said to his father: 'Dear father, to whom wilt thou give me?'

He said it a second and a third time. Then the father replied angrily: 'I shall give thee unto Death.'

(The father, having once said so, though in haste, Had to be true to his word and to sacrifice his son.)

The son said: 'I go as the first, at the head of many who have still to die; I go in the midst of many who are now dying. What will be the work of Yama, the ruler of the departed, which today he has to do unto me?

'Look back how it was with those who came before, look forward how it will be with those who come hereafter. A mortal ripens like corn, like corn he springs up again.'

(Nachiketas enters into the abode of Yama Vaivasvata, and there is no one to receive him. Thereupon one of the attendants of Yama is supposed to say:)

'Fire enters into the houses, when a Brahmin enters as a guest. That fire is quenched by this peace-offering—bring water, O Vaivasvata! .

'A Brahamin that dwells in the house of a foolish man without receiving food to eat, destroys his hopes and expectations, his possessions, his righteousness, his sacred and his good deeds, and all his sons and cattle.'

(Yama, returning to his house after an absence of three nights, during which time Nachiketas had received no hospitality from him, says:)

'O Brahmin, as thou, a venerable guest, hast dwelt in my house three nights without eating, therefore choose now three boons. Hail to thee! and welfare to me!'

Nachiketas said: '0 Death, as the first of the three boons I choose that Gautama, my father, be pacified, kind, and free from anger towards me; 'and that he may know me and greet me, when I shall have been dismissed by thee.'

Yama said: 'Through my favour Auddalaki Aruni, thy father, will know thee, and be again towards thee freed from the mouth of death.'

Nachiketas said: 'In the heaven-world there is no fear; thou art not there, O Death, and no one is afraid on account of old age. Leaving behind both hunger and thirst, and out of the reach of sorrow, all rejoice in the world of heaven.'

'Thou knowest, O Death, the fire-sacrifice which leads us to heaven; tell it to me, for I am full of faith. Those who live in the heaven-world reach immortality,-this I ask as my— second boon.'

Yama said: 'I tell it thee, learn it from me, and when thou understandest that fire-sacrifice which leads to heaven, know, 0 Nachiketas, that it is the attainment of the endless worlds, and their firm support, hidden in darkness.'

Yama then told him that fire-sacrifice, the beginning of all the worlds, and what bricks are required for the altar, and how many, and how they are to be placed. And Nachiketas repeated all as it had been told to him. The Mrityu, being pleased with him, said again:

The generous, being satisfied, said to him :'1 give thee now another boon; that fire-sacrifice shall be named after thee, take also this many-coloured chain.'

'He who has three times performed this Nachiketa rite, and has been united with the three father, mother, and teacher,' and has performed the three duties study, sacrifice, almsgiving, overcomes birth and death. When he has learnt and understood this fire, which knows or makes us know all that is born of Brahman, which is venerable and divine, then he obtains everlasting peace.

'He who knows the three Nachiketa fires, and knowing the three, piles up the Nachiketa sacrifice, he, having first thrown off the chains of death, rejoices in the world of heaven, beyond the reach of grief.'

'This, O Nachiketas, is thy fire which leads to heaven, and which thou hast chosen as thy second boon. That fire all men will proclaim. Choose now, O Nachiketas, thy third boon.'

Nachiketas said: 'There is that doubt, when a man is dead, some saying, he is; others, he is not. This I should like to know, taught by thee; this is the third of my boons.'

Death said: 'On this point even the gods have doubted formerly; it is not easy to understand. That subject is subtle. Choose another boon, O Nachiketas, do not press me, and let me off that boon.'

Nachiketas said: 'On this point even the gods have doubed indeed, and thou, Death, hast declared it to be not easy to understand, and another teacher like thee is not to be found:—surely no other boon is like unto this.'

Death said: 'Choose sons and grandsons who shall live a hundred years, herds of cattle, elephants, gold, and horses. Choose the wide abode of the earth, and live thyself as many harvests as thou desirest.'

'If you can think of any boon equal to that, choose wealth and long life. Be king, Nachiketas, on the wide earth. I make thee the enjoyer of all desires.

'Whatever desires are difficult to attain among mortals, ask for them according to thy wish;—these fair maidens with their chariots and musical instruments,—such are indeed not to be obtained by men,—be waited on by them whom I give to thee, but do not ask me about dying.'

Nachiketas said: 'These things last till tomorrow, O Death, for they wear out this vigour of all the senses. Even the whole of life is short. Keep thou thy horses, keep dance and song for thyself.

'No man can be made happy by wealth. Shall we possess wealth, when we see thee? Shall we live, as long as thou rulest? Only that boon which I have chosen is to be chosen by me.'

'What mortal, slowly decaying here below, and knowing, after having approached them, the freedom from decay enjoyed by the immortals, would delight in a long life, after he has pondered on the pleasures which arise from beauty and love?

'No, that on which there is this doubt, O Death, tell us what there is in that great Hereafter. Nachiketas does not choose another boon but that which enters into the hidden world.'

•

Death said: 'The good is one thing, the pleasant another; these two, having different objects, chain a man. It is well with him who clings to the good; he who chooses the pleasant, misses his end.

'The good and the pleasant approach man: the wise goes round about them and distinguishes them. Yea, the wise prefers the good to the pleasant, but the fool chooses the pleasant through greed and avarice.

'Thou, O Nachiketas, after pondering all pleasures that are or seem delightful, hast dismissed them all. Thou hast not gone into the road that leadeth to wealth, in which many men perish.

'Wide apart and leading to different points are these two, ignorance, and what is known as wisdom. I believe Nachiketas to be one who desires knowledge, for even many pleasures did not tear thee away.

'Fools dwelling in darkness, wise in their own conceit, and puffed up with vain knowledge, go round and round, staggering to and from, like blind men led by the blind.

'The Hereafter never rises before the eyes of the careless child, deluded by the delusion of wealth. "This is the world," he thinks, "there is no other;" -thus he falls again and again' under my sway.

'He the Self of whom many are not even able to hear, whom many, even when they hear of him, do not comprehend; wonderful is a man, when found, who is able to teach him the Self; wonderful is he who comprehends him, when taught by an able teacher.

'That Self, when taught by an inferior man, is not easy to be known, even though often thought upon; unless it be taught by another, there is no way to it, for it is inconceivably smaller than what is small.

'That doctrine is not to be obtained by argument, but when it is declared by another, then, O dearest, it is easy to understand. Thou hast obtained it now; thou art truly a man of true resolve. May we have always an inquirer like thee!'

Nachiketas said: 'I know that what is called a treasure is transient, for that eternal is not obtained by things which are not eternal. Hence the Nachiketa fire-sacrifice has been laid by me first; then, by means of transient things, I have obtained what is not transient (the teaching of Yama).'

Yama said: 'Though thou hadst seen the fulfilment of all desires, the foundation of the world, the endless rewards of good deeds, the shore where there is no fear, that which is magnified by praise, the wide abode, the rest, yet being wise thou hast with firm resolve dismissed it all.

'The wise who, by means of meditation on his Self, recognises the Ancient, who is difficult to be seen, who has entered into the dark, who is hidden in the cave, who dwells in the abyss, as God, he indeed leaves joy and sorrow far behind.

'A mortal who has heard this and embraced it, who has separated from it all qualities, and has thus reached the subtle Being, rejoices, because he has obtained what is a cause for rejoicing. The house of Brahman is open, I believe, O Nachiketas.'

Naichketas said: 'That which thou seest as neither this nor that, as neither effect nor cause, as neither past nor future, tell me that.'

Yama said: 'That word or place which all the Vedas record, which all penances proclaim, which men desire when they live as religious students, that word I tell thee briefly, it is Om.

'That imperishable syllable means Brahman, that syllable means the highest Brahmin; he who knows that syllable, whatever he desires, is his.

'This is the best support, this is the highest support; he who knows that support is magnified in the world of Brahman.

'The knowing Self is not born, it dies not; it sprang from nothing, nothing sprang from it. the Ancient is unborn, eternal, everlasting; he is not killed, though the body is killed.

'If the killer thinks that he kills, if the killed thinks that he is killed, they do not understand; for this one does not kill, nor is that one killed.

'The Self, smaller than small, greater than great, is hidden in the heart of that creature. A man who is free from desires and free from grief, sees the majesty of the Self by the grace of the Creator.

'Though sitting still, he walks far; though lying down, he goes everywhere. Who, save myself, is able to know that god who rejoices and rejoices not?

'The wise who knows the Self as bodiless within the bodies, as unchanging among changing things, as great and omnipresent, does never grieve.

'That Self cannot be gained by the Veda, nor by undestanding, nor by much learning. He who the Self chooses, by him the Self can be gained. The Self chooses him 'his body' as his own.

'But he who has not first turned away from his wickedness, who is not tranquil, and subdued, or whose mind is not at rest, he can never obtain the Self even by knowledge.

'Who then knows where He is, He to whom the Brahmins and Kshatriyas are as it were, but food, and death itself a condiment?'

•

'There are the two, drinking their reward in the world of the own works, entered into the cave of the heart, dwelling on the highest summit the ether in the heart. Those who know Brahman call them shade and light; likewise, those householders who perform the Trinachiketa sacrifice.

'May we be able to master that Nachiketa rite which is a bridge for sacrificers; also that which is the highest, imperishable Brahman for those who wish to cross over to the fearless shore.

'Know the Self to be sitting in the chariot, the body to be the chariot, the intellect *(buddhi)* the charioteer, and the mind the reins.

'The senses they call the horses, the objects of the senses their roads. When he "the Highest Self" is in union with the body, the senses, and the mind, then wise people call him the Enjoyer.

'He who has no understanding and whose mind 'the reins' is never firmly held, his senses "horses" are unmanageable, like vicious horses of a charioteer.

'But he who has understanding and whose mind is always firmly held, his senses are under control, like good horses of a charioteer.

'He who has no understanding, who is unmindful and always impure, never reaches that place, but enters into the round of births.

'But he who has understanding, who is mindful and always pure, reaches indeed that place, from whence he is not born again.

'But who has understanding for his charioteer, and who holds the reins of the mind, he reaches the end of his journey, and that is the highest place of Vishnu.

'Beyond the senses there are the objects, beyond the objects there is the mind, beyond the mind there is the intellect, the Great Self is beyond the intellect.

'Beyond the Great there is the Undeveloped, beyond the Undeveloped there is the Person (Purusha). Beyond the Person there is nothing—this is the goal, the highest road.

'That Self is hidden in all beings and does not shine forth, but it is seen by subtle seers through their sharp and subtle intellect.

'A wise man should keep down speech and mind; he should keep them within the Self which is knowledge; he should keep knowledge within the Self which is the Great; and he should keep the Great within the Self which is the Quiet.

'Rise, awake! having obtained your boons, understand them! The sharp edge of a razor is difficult to pass over; thus the wise say the path to the Self is hard.

'He who had perceived that which is without sound, without touch, without form, without decay, without taste, eternal, without smell, without beginning, without end, beyond the Great, and Unchangeable, is freed from the jaws of death.

'A wise man who has repeated or heard the ancient story of Nachiketas told by Death, is magnified in the field of Brahman.

'And he who repeats this greatest mystery in an assembly of Brahmins, or full of devotion at the time of the Sraddha sacrifice, obtains thereby infinite rewards.'

(2)

Death said: 'The Self-existent pierced the openings of the senses so that they turn forward: therefore man looks forward, not backward into himself. Some wise man, however, with his eyes closed and wishing for immortality, saw the Self behind.

'Children follow after outward pleasures, and fall into the snare of widespread death. Wise men only, knowing the nature of what is immortal, do not look for anything stable here among things unstable.

'That by which we know form, taste, smell, sounds, and loving touches, by that also we know what exists besides. This is that which thou hast asked for.

'The wise, when he knows that that by which he perceives all objects in sleep or in waking is the great omnipresent Self, grieves no more.

'He who knows this living soul which eats honey (preceives objects) as being the Self, always near, the Lord of the past and the future, henceforward fears no more. This is that.

'He who knows him who was born first from the brooding heat for he was born before the water, who, entering into the heart, abides therein, and was perceived from the elements. This is that.

'He who knows Aditi also, who is one with all deities, who arises with Prana (breath or Hiranyagarbha), who, entering into the heart, abides therein, and was born from the elements. This is that.

'There is Agni (fire), the all-seeing, hidden in the two fire-sticks, well-guarded like a child in the womb by the mother, day after day to be adored by men when they awake and bring oblations. This is that.

'And that whence the sun rises, and whither it goes to set, there all the Devas are contained, and no one goes beyond. This is that.

'What is here visible in the world, the same is there invisible in Brahman; and what is there, the same is here. He who sees any difference here between Brahman and the world, goes from death to death.

'Even by the mind this Brahman is to be obtained, and then there is no difference whatsoever. He goes from death to death who sees any difference here.

'The Person Purusha, of the size of a thumb, stands in the middle of the Self, as lord of the past and the future, and henceforward fears no more. This is that.

'That Person, of the size of a thumb, is like a light without smoke, lord of the past and the future, he is the same today and tomorrow. This is that.

'As rain-water that has fallen on a mountain-ridge runs down the rocks on all sides, thus does he, who sees a difference between qualities, run after them on all sides.

'As pure water poured into pure water remains the same, thus, O Gautama, is the Self of a thinker who knows.'

•

'There is a town with eleven gates belonging to the Unborn Brahman, whose thoughts are never crooked. He who approaches it, grieves no more, and liberated from all bonds of ignorance becomes free. This is that.

'The Brahman is the swan (sun), dwelling in the bright heaven; he is the Vasu (air), dwelling in the sky, he is the sacrificer (fire), dwelling on the hearth; he is the guest, Soma, dwelling in the sacrificial jar; he dwells in men, in gods *(vara),* in the sacrifice *(rita),* in heaven; he is born in the water, on earth, in the sacrifice *(rita),* on the mountains; he is the True and the Great.

'The Brahman it is who sends up the breath (Prana), and who throws back the breath (Apana). All the Devas (senses) worship him, the adorable, or the dwarf, who sits in the centre.'

'When that Brahman, who dwells in the body, is tom away and freed from the body, what remains then? This is that.

'No mortal lives by the breath that goes up and by the breath that goes down. We live by another, in whom these two repose.

'Well then, O Gautama, I shall tell thee this mystery, the old Brahman, and what happens to the Self, after reaching death.

'Some enter the womb in order to have a body, as organic beings, others go into inorganic matter, according to their work and according to their knowledge.

'He, the highest Person, who is awake in us while we are asleep, shaping one lovely sight after another, that indeed is the Bright, that is Brahman, that alone is called the Immortal. All worlds are contained in it, and no one goes beyond. This is that.

'As the one fire, after it has entered the world, though one, becomes different according to whatever it burns, thus the one Self within all things becomes different, according to whatever it enters, and exists also without.

'As the one air, after it has entered the world, though one, becomes different according to whatever it enters, thus the one Self within all things becomes different, according to whatever it enters, and exists also without.

'As the sun, the eye of the whole world, is not contaminated by the external impurities seen by the eyes, thus the one Self within all things is never contaminated by the misery of the world, being himself without.

'There is one ruler, the Self within all things, who makes the one form manifold. The wise who perceive him within their Self to them belongs eternal happiness, not to others.

'There is one eternal thinker, thinking non-eternal thoughts, who, though one, fulfils the desires of many. The wise who perceive him within their Self to them belongs eternal peace, not others.

'They perceive that highest indescribable pleasure, saying, This is that. How then can I undersand it? Has it its own light, or does it reflect light?

'The sun does not shine there, nor the moon and the stars, nor these lightnings, and much less this fire. When he shines, everyithing shines after him; by his light all this is lighted.'

•

'There is that ancient tree, whose roots grow upward and whose branches grow downward;—that indeed is called the Bright, that is called Brahman, that alone is called the Immortal. All worlds are contained in it, and no one goes beyond. This is that.

'Whatever there is, the whole world, when gone forth from the Brahman, trembles in its breath. That Brahman is a great terror, like a drawn sword. Those who know it become immortal.

'From terror of Brahman fire bums, from terror the sun burns, from terror Indra and Vayu, and Death, as the fifth, run away.

'If a man could not understand it before the falling asunder of his body, then he has to take body again in the worlds of creation.

'As in a mirror, so Brahman may be seen clearly here in this body; as in a dream, in the world of the Fathers; as in the water, he is seen about in the world of the Gandharvas; as in light and shade, in the world of Brahman.

'Having understood that the senses are distinct from the Atman, and that their rising and setting, their waking and sleeping, belongs to them in their distinct existence and not to the Atman, a wise man grieves no more.

'Beyond the senses is the mind, beyond the mind is the highest created Being, higher than that Being is the Great Self, higher than the Great, the highest Undeveloped.

'Beyond the Undeveloped is the Person, the all-pervading and entirely imperceptible. Every creature that knows him is liberated, and obtains immortaility.

'His form is not to be seen, no one beholds him with the eye. He is imagined by the heart, by wisdom, by the mind. Those who know this, are immortal.

'When the five instruments of knowledge stand still together with the mind, and when the intellect does not move, that is called the highest state.

'This, the firm holding back of the senses, is what is called Yoga. He must be free from thoughtlessness then, for Yoga comes and goes.

'He, the Self, cannot be reached by speech, by mind, or by the eye. How can it be apprehended except by him who says: "He is?"

'By the words "He is," is he to be apprehended, and by admitting the reality of both, the invisible Brahman and the visible world, as comming from Brahman. When he has been apprehended by the words "He is," then his reality reveals itself.

'When all desires that dwell in his heart cease, then the mortal becomes immortal, and obtains Brahman.

'When all the ties of the heart are severed here on earth, then the mortal becomes immortal—here ends the teaching.

'There are a hundred and one arteries of the heart, one of them penetrates the crown of the head. Moving upwards by it, a man at his death reaches the Immortal; the other arteries serve for departing in different directions.

'The Person not larger than a thumb, the inner Self, is always settled in the heart of men. Let a man draw that Self forth from his body with steadiness, as one draws the pith from reed. Let him know that Self as the Bright, as the Immortal; yes, as the Bright, as the Immortal.'

He having received this knowledge taught by Death and the whole rule of Yoga, Nachiketa became free from passion and death, and obtained Brahman. Thus it will be with another also who knows thus what relates to the Self.

May He protect us both! May He enjoy us both! May we acquire strength together! May our knowledge become bright! May we never quarrel! Om! Peace! peace! peace!

Mundaka Upanishad

The Way of the Monk

'Mundaka' means the monks who have shaven their heads clean—and as such the Upanishad is believed to have belonged to them, and it has been one of the most popular Upanishad. It presents the next step from the religion of the Vedas, based on Yajnas and rishis who were householders, to the religion of tapas practised by celibate monks. It deals with the newly devised stages of the knowledge of Brahman, its doctrine and the way to attain it.

[1]

Brahma was the first of the Devas, the maker of the universe, the preserver of the world. He told the knowledge of Brahman, the foundation of all knowledge, to his eldest son Atharvan.

Whatever Brahma told Atharvan, that knowledge of Brahman Atharvan formerly told to Angir; he told it to Satyavaha Bharadvaja, and Bharadvaja told it in succession to Angiras.

Shaunaka, the great householder, approached Angiras respectfully and asked: 'Sir, what is that through which, if it is known, everything else becomes known?'

He said to him: 'Two kinds of knowledge must be known, this is what all who know Brahman tell us, the higher and the lower knowledge.

'The lower knowledge is the Rigveda, Yajurveda, Samaveda, Atharvaveda, Shiksha (phonetics), Kalpa (ceremonial), Vyakarana (grammar), Nirukta (etymology), Chhandas (metre), Jyotisha (astronomy); but the higher knowledge is that by which the Indestructible Brahman is apprehended.

'That which cannot be seen, nor seized, which has no family and no caste, no eyes nor ears, no hands nor feet, the eternal, the omnipresent, allpervading, infinitesimal, that which is imperishable, that it is which the wise regard as the source of all beings.

'As the spider sends forth and draws in its thread, as plants grow on the earth, as from every man hairs spring forth on the head and the body, thus does everything arise here from the Indestructible.

'The Brahman swells by means of brooding (Tapa) hence is produced matter (food); from matter breath, mind, the true (Satya), the worlds (seven), and from the works formed by men in the worlds, the immortal, the eternal effects, rewards, and punishments of works.

'From him who perceives all and who knows all, whose brooding consists of knowledge, from the highest Brahman is born that Brahman, name, form, and matter (food).'

•

This is the truth: the sacrificial works which the poets saw in the hymns of the Veda have been performed in many ways in the Treta age. Practise them diligently, ye lovers of truth, this is your path that leads to the world of good works!

When the fire is lighted and the flame flickers, let a man offer his oblations between the two portions of melted butter, as an offering with faith.

If a man's Agnihotra sacrifice is not followed by the new-moon and full-moon sacrifices, by the four-months' sacrifices, and by the harvest sacrifice, if it is unattended by guests, not offered at all, or without the Vaishvadeva ceremony, or not offered according to rule, then it destroys his seven worlds.

Kali (black), Karali (terrific), Manojava (swift as thought), Sulohit (very red), Sudhumravarna (purple), Sphulingini (sparkling), all these playing about are called the seven tongues of fire.

If a man performs his sacred words when these flames are shining, and the oblations follow at the right time, then they lead him as sun-rays to where the one Lord of the Devas dwells.

Come hither, come hither! the brilliant oblations say to him, and carry the sacrificer on the rays of the sun, while they utter pleasant speech and praise him, saying: 'This is thy holy Brahma-world (Svarga), gained by thy good works.'

But frail, in truth, are those boats, the sacrifices, the eighteen, in which this lower ceremonial has been told. Fools who praise this as the highest good, are subject again and again to old age and death.

Fools dwelling in darkness, wise in their own conceit, and puffed up with vain knowledge, go round and round staggering to and fro, like blind men led by the blind.

Children, when they have long lived in ignorance, consider themselves happy. Because those who depend on their good works are, owing to their passions, improvident, they fall and become miserable when their life in the world which they had gained by their good works is finished.

Considering sacrifice and good works as the best, these fools know no higher good, and having enjoyed their reward on the height of heaven, gained by good works, they enter again this world or a lower one.

But those who practise penance and faith in the forest, tranquil, wise, and living on alms, depart free from passion through the sun to where that immortal Person (Purusha) dwells whose nature is imperishable.

Let a Brahmin, after he has examined all these worlds which are gained by works, acquire freedom from all desires. Nothing that is eternal (not made) can be gained by what is not eternal (made). Let him, in order to understand this, take fuel in his hand and approach a Guru who is learned and dwells entirely in Brahman.

To that pupil who has approached him respectfully, whose thoughts are not troubled by any desires, and who has obtained perfect peace, the wise teacher truly told that knowledge of Brahman through which knows the eternal and true Person.

(2)

This is the truth. As from a blazing fire sparks, being like unto fire, fly forth a thousandfold, thus are various beings brought forth from the Imperishable, my friend, and return thither also.

That heavenly Person is without body, he is both without and within, not produced, without breath and without mind, pure, higher than the high, Imperishable.

From him when entering on creation, is born breath, mind, and all organs of sense, ether, air, light, water, and the earth, the support of all.

Fire (the sky) is his head, his eyes the sun and the moon, the quarters his ears, his speech the Vedas disclosed, the wind his breath, his heart the universe; from his feet came the earth; he is indeed the inner Self of all things.

From him comes Agni (fire), the sun being the fuel; from the moon (Soma) comes rain (Parjanya); from the earth herbs; and man gives seed unto the woman. Thus many beings are begotten from the Person.

From him come the Rik, the Saman, the Yajus, the Diksha (initiatory rites), all sacrifices and offerings of animals, and the fees bestowed on priests, the year, too, the sacrificer, and the worlds, in which the moon shines brightly and the sun.

From him the many Devas too are begotten, the Sadhyas (genii), men, cattle, birds, the up and down breathings, rice and corn for sacrifices, penance, faith, truth, abstinence, and law.

The seven senses (Prana) also spring from him, the seven lights (acts of sensation), the seven kinds of fuel (objects by which the senses are lighted), the seven sacrifices results of sensation, these seven worlds (the places of the senses, the worlds determined by the senses) in which the senses move, which rest in the cave of the heart, and are placed there seven and seven.

Hence come the seas and all the mountains, from him flow the rivers of every kind; hence come all herbs and the juice through which the inner Self subsists with the elements.

The Person is all this, sacrifice, penance, Brahman, the highest immortal; he who knows this hidden in the cave of the heart, he, O friend, scatters the knot of ignorance here on earth.

•

Manifest, near, moving in the cave of the heart is the great Being. In it everything is centred which ye know as moving, breathing, and blinking, as being and not-being, as adorable, as the best, that is beyond the understanding of creatures.

That which is brilliant, smaller than small, that on which the worlds are founded and their inhabitants, that is the indestructible Brahman, that is the breath, speech, mind; that is the true, that is the immortal. that is to be hit. Hit it, O friend!

Having taken the Upanishad as the bow, as the great weapon, let him place on it the arrow, sharpened by devotion! Then having drawn it with a thought directed to that which is, hit the mark, O friend, that which is the Indestructible!

Om is the bow, the Self is the arrow, Brahman is called its aim. It is to be hit by a man who is not thoughtless; and then, as the arrow becomes one with the target, he will become one with Brahman.

In him the heaven, the earth, and the sky are woven, the mind also with all the senses. Know him alone as the Self, and leave off other worlds! He is the bridge of the Immortal.

He moves about becoming manifold within the heart where the arteries meet, like spokes fastened to the nave. Meditate on the Self as Om! Hail to you, that you may cross beyond the sea of darkness!

He who understands all and who knows all, he to whom all this glory in the world belongs, the Self, is placed in the ether, in the heavenly city of Brahman 'the heart'. He assumes the nature of mind, and becomes the guide of the body of the senses. He subsists in food, in close proximity to the heart. The wise who understand this, behold the Immortal which shines forth full of bliss.

The fetter of the heart is broken, all doubts are solved, all his works and their effects perish when He has been beheld who is high and low (cause and effect).

In the highest golden sheath there is the Brahman without passions and without parts. That is pure, that is the light of lights, that is it which they know who know the Self.

The sun does not shine there, nor the moon and the stars, nor these lightnings, and much less this fire. When he shines, everything shines after him; by his light all this is lighted.

That immortal Brahman is right and left. It has gone forth below and above; Brahman alone is all this, it is the best.

(3)

Two birds, inseparable friends, cling to the same tree. One of them eats the sweet fruit, the other looks on without eating.

On the same tree man sits grieving, immersed, bewildered by his own impotence (Anisa). But when he sees the other lord (Isa) contented and knows his glory, then his grief passes away.

When the seer sees the brilliant maker and lord of the world as the Person who has his source in Brahman, then he is wise, and shaking off good and evil, he reaches the highest oneness, free from passions.

For he is the Breath shining forth in all beings, and he who understands this becomes truly wise, not a talker only. He revels in the Self, he delights in the Self, and having performed his works, truthfulness, penance, meditation, etc., he rests, firmly established in Brahman, the best of those who know Brahman.

By truthfulness, indeed, by penance, right knowledge, and abstinence must that Self be gained; the Self whom spotless anchorites gain is pure, and like a light within the body.

The true prevails, not the untrue; by the true the path is laid out, the way of the gods, Devayana, on which the sages, satisfied in their desires, proceed to where there is that highest place of the True One. That true Brahman shines forth, grand, divine, inconceivable, smaller than small; it is far beyond what is far and yet near here, it is hidden in the cave of the heart among those who see it even here.

He is not apprehended by the eye, nor by speech, nor by the other senses, nor by penance or good works. When a man's nature has become purified by the serene light of knowledge, then he sees him, meditating on him as without parts.

That subtle Self is to be known by thought (Chetas) there where breath has entered fivefold; for every thought of men is interwoven with the senses, and when thought is purified, then the Self arises.

Whatever state a man whose nature is purified imagines, and whatever desires he desires for himself or for others, that state he conquers and those desires he obtains. Therefore let every man who desires happiness worship the man who knows the Self.

•

He the knower of the Self knows that highest home of Brahman, in which all is contained and shines brightly. The wise who without desiring happiness, worship that Person, transcend this seed, they are not born again.

He who forms desires in his mind, is born again through his desires here and there. But to him whose desires are fulfilled and who is conscious of the true Self within himself all desires vanish, even here on earth.

That Self cannot be gained by the Veda, nor by understanding, nor by much learning. He whom the Self chooses, by him the Self can be gained. The Self chooses him 'his body' as his own.

Nor is that Self to be gained by one who is destitute of strength, or without earnestness, or without right meditation. But if a wise man strives after it by those means, by strength, earnestness, and right meditation, then his Self enters the home of Brahman.

When they have reached him, the Self, the sages become satisfied through knowledge, they are conscious of their Self, their passions have passed away, and they are tranquil. The wise, having reached Him who is ominipresent everywhere, devoted to the Self, enter into him wholly.

Having well ascertained the object of the knowledge of the Vedanta, and having purified their nature by the Yoga of renunciation, all anchorites, enjoying the highest immortality, become free at the time of the great end 'death' in the worlds of Brahma.

Their fifteen parts enter into their elements, their Devas, the senses, into their corresponding Devas. Their deeds and their Self with all his knowledge become all one in the highest Imperishable.

As the flowing rivers disappear in the sea, losing their name and their form, thus a wise man, freed from name and form, goes to the divine Person, who is greater than the great.

He who knows that highest Brahman, becomes even Brahman. In his race no one is born ignorant of Brahman. He overcomes grief, he overcomes evil; free from the fetters of the heart, he becomes immortal.

And this is declared by the following Rik verse: 'Let a man tell this science of Brahman to those only who have performed all necessary acts, who are versed in the Vedas, and firmly established in the lower Brahman, who themselves offer as oblation the one Rishi (Agni), full of faith and by whom the rite of carrying fire on the head has been perfomed, according to the rule of the Atharvanas.'

The Rishi Angiras formerly told this true science to Saunaka; a man who has not performed the proper rites, does not read it. Adoration to the highest Rishis! Adoration to the highest Rishis!

Prashna Upanishad

Everything is fixed in Prana

This interesting Upanishad deals in six questions put by six seekers of Brahman to the sage Pippalada: origin of matter and the life of Prajapati; the role of Prana in activating life forces; Prana in human beings; aspects of sleep, light and deep. meditation on Om; and the parts of human beings. The concepts of Pitriyana and Devayana are also presented. The ideas are unique to Indian thought.

First Question

Adoration to the Highest Self! Harih Om!

Sukeshas Bharadvaja, and Shaivya Satyakama, and Sauryayanin Gargya, and Kausalya Ashvalayana, and Bhargava Vaidarbhi, and Kabandhin Katyayana, these were devoted to Brahman, firm in Brahman, seeking for the Highest Brahman. They thought that the venerable Pippalada could tell them all that, and they therefore took fuel in their hands like pupils, and approached him.

That Rishi said to them: 'Stay there a year longer, with penance, abstinence, and faith; then you may ask questions according to your pleasure, and if we know them, we shall tell you all.'

Then, after the year was over, Kabandhin Katyayana approached him and asked: 'Sir, from whence may these creatures be born?'

He replied: 'Prajapati, the lord of creatures, was desirous of creatures. He performed penance, and having performed penance, he produced a pair, matter *(rayi)* and spirit (Prana), thinking that they together should produce creatures for him in many ways.

'The sun is spirit, matter is the moon. All this, what has body and what has no body, is matter, and therefore body indeed is matter.

'Now Aditya, the sun, when he rises, goes toward the East, and thus receives the Eastern spirits into his rays. And when he illuminates the South, the West, the North, the Zenith, the Nadir, the intermediate quarters, and everything he thus receives all spirits into his rays.

'Thus he rises, as Vaishvanara, belonging to all men, assuming all forms, as spirit, as fire. This has been said in the following verse:

"They knew him who assumes all forms, the golden, who knows all things, who ascends highest, alone in his splendours, and warms us; the thousand-rayed, who abides in a hundred places, the spirit of all creatures, the Sun, rises."

'The year indeed is Prajapati, and there are two paths thereof, the Southern and the Northern. Now those who here believe in sacrifices and pious gifts as work done, gain the moon only as their future world, and return again. Therefore the Rishis who desire offspring, go to the South, and that path of the Fathers is matter *(rayi).*

'But those who have sought the Self by penance, abstinence, faith, and knowledge, gain by the Northern path Aditya, the sun. This is the home of the spirits, the immortal, free from danger, the highest. From thence they do not return, for it is the end. Thus says the Shloka:

"Some call him the father with five feet (the five seasons), and with twelve shapes (the twelve months), the giver of rain in the highest half of heaven; others again say that the sage is placed in the lower half, in the chariot wheels and six spokes."

'The month is Prajapati; its dark half is matter, its bright half spirit. Therefore some Rishis perform sacrifice in the bright half others in the other half.

'Day and Night are Prajapati; its day is spirit, its night matter. Those who unite in love by day waste their spirit, but to unite in love by night is right.

'Food is Prajapati. Hence proceeds seed, and from it these creatures are born.

'Those therefore who observe this rule of Prajapati, produce a pair, and to them belongs this Brahma-world here. But those in whom dwell penance, abstinence, and truth,

'To them belongs that pure Brahma-world, to them, namely, in whom there is nothing crooked~ nothing false, and no guile.'

Second Question

Then Bhargava Vaidarbhi asked him: 'Sir, How many gods keep what has thus been created, how many manifest this, and who is the best of them?'

He replied: 'The ether is that god, the wind, fire, water, earth, speech, mind, eye, and ear. These, when they have manifested their power, contend and say: We each of us support this body and keep it.

'Then Prana, breath, spirit, life, as the best, said to them: Be not deceived, I alone, dividing myself fivefold, support this body and keep it.

'They were incredulous; so he, from pride, did as if he were going out from above. Thereupon, as he went out, all the others went out, and as he returned, all the others returned. As bees go out when their queen goes out, and return when she returns, thus did speech, mind, eye, and ear; and, being satisfied, they praised Prana, saying:

'He is Agni (fire), he shines as Surya (sun), he is Parjanya (rain), the powerful (Indra), he is Vayu (wind), he is the

earth, he is matter, he is God—he is what is not, and what is immortal.

'As spokes in the nave of a wheel, everything is fixed in Prana, the verses of the Rigveda, Yajurveda, Samaveda the sacrifice, the Kshatriyas, and the Brahmins.

'As Prajapati, lord of creatures, thou movest about in the womb, thou indeed art born again. To thee, the Prana, these creatures bring offerings, to thee who dwellest with the other Pranas the organs of sense.

Thou art the best carrier for the Gods, thou art the fires offering to the Fathers. Thou art the true work of the Rishis, of the Atharvangiras.

'O Prana, thou art Indra by thy light, thou art Rudra, as a protector; thou movest in the sky, thou art the sun, the lord of lights.

'When thou showerest down rain, then, O Prana, these creatures of thine are delighted, hoping that there will be food, as much as they desire.

'Thou art a Vratya, O Prana, the only Rishi, the consumer of everything, the good lord. We are the givers of what thou hast to consume, thou, O Matarisvan, art our father.

'Make propitious that body of thine which dwells in speech, in the ear, in the eye, and which pervades the mind; do not go away!

'All this is in the power of Prana, whatever exists in the three heavens. Protect us like a mother her sons, and give us happiness and wisdom.'

Third Question

Then Kausalya Ashvalayana asked: 'Sir, whence is that Prana (spirit) born? How does it come into this body? And how does it abide after it has divided itself? How does it go out? How does it support what is without, and how what is within?'

He replied: 'You ask questions more difficult, but you are very fond of Brahman, therefore I shall tell it to you.

'This Prana is born of the Self. Like the shadow thrown on a man, this Prana is spread out over the Brahman. By the work of the mind does it come into this body.

'As a king commands officials, saying to them: Rule these villages or those, so does that Prana dispose the other Pranas, each for their separate work.

'The Apana, the down-breathing, in the organs of excretion and generation; the Prana himself dwells in the eye and ear, passing through mouth and nose. In the middle is the Samana, the onbreathing; it carries what has been sacrificed as food equally over the body, and the seven lights proceed from it.

'The Self is in the heart. There are the 101 arteries, and in each of them there are a hundred smaller veins, and for each of these branches there are 72,000. In these the Vyana, the backbreathing, moves.

'Through one of them, the Udana, the out-breathing, leads us upwards to the good world by good work, to the bad world by bad work, to the world of men by both.

'The sun rises as the external Prana for it assists the Prana in the eye. The deity that exists in the earth, is there in support of man's Apana, downbreathing. The ether between sun and earth is the Samana, onbreathing, the air is Vyana, backbreathing.

'Light is the Udana, outbreathing, and therefore he whose light has gone out comes to a new birth with his senses absorbed in the mind.

'Whatever his thought at the time of death, with that he goes back to Prana, united with light, together with the Jivatma leads on to the world, as deserved.

'He who, thus knowing, knows Prana, his offspring does not perish, and he becomes immortal. Thus says the Shloka:

'He who has known the origin, the entry, the place, the fivefold distribution, and the internal state of the Prana, obtains immortality, yes, obtains immortality.'

Fourth Question

Then Sauryayanin Gargya asked: 'Sir, what are they that sleep in this man, and what are they that are awake in him? What power (deva) is it that sees dreams? Whose is the happiness? On what do all these depend?'

He replied: 'O Gargya, As all the rays of the sun, when it sets, are gathered up in that disc of light, and as they, when the sun rises again and again, come forth, so is all this (all the senses) gathered up in the highest faculty deva, the mind. Therefore, at that time that man does not hear, see, smell, taste, touch; he does not speak, he does not take, does not enjoy, does not evacuate, does not move about. He sleeps, that is what people say.

'The fires of the Pranas are, as it were, awake in that town (the body). The Apana is the Garhapatya fire, the Vyana the Anvaharyapachana fire; and because it is taken out of the Garhapatya fire, which is fire for taking out, therefore the Prana is the Ahavaniya fire.

'Because it carries equally these two oblations, the outbreathing and the inbreathing, the Saman is he, the Hotri priest. The mind is the sacrificer, the Udana is the reward of the sacrifice, and it leads the sacrificer every day in deep sleep to Brahman.

'There that god, the mind, enjoys in sleep greatness. What has been seen, he sees again; what has been heard, he hears again; what has been enjoyed in different countries and quarters, he enjoys again; what has been seen and not seen, heard and not heard, enjoyed and not enjoyed, he sees it all; he, being all, sees.

'And when he is overpowered by light, then that god sees no dreams, and at that time that happiness arises in his body.

'And, O friend, as birds go to a tree to roost, thus all this rests in the Highest Atman,—

'The earth and its subtile elements, the water and its subtile elements, the light and its subtile elements, the air and its subtile elments, the ether and its subtile elements; the eye and what can be seen, the ear and what can be heard, the nose and what can be smelled, the taste and what can be tasted, the skin and what can be touched, the voice and what can be spoken, the hands and what can be grasped, the feet and what can be walked, the mind and what can be perceived, intellect (Buddhi) and what can be conceived, personality and what can be personified, thought and what can be thought, light and what can be lighted up, the Prana and what is to be supported by it.

'For he it is who sees, hears, smells, tastes, perceives, conceives, acts, he whose essence is knowledge, the Person, and he dwells in the highest, indestructible Self.

'He who knows that indestructible being, obtains what is the highest and indestructible, he without a shadow, without a body, without colour, bright,—yes, O friends, he who knows it, becomes all-knowing, becomes all. On this there is this Shloka:

''He, a friend, who knows that indestructible being wherein the true knower, the vital spirits (Pranas), together with all the powers (deva), and the elements rest, he being all-knowing, has penetrated all.''

Fifth Question

Then Shaivya Satyakama asked him: 'Sir, if some one among men should meditate here until death on the syllable Om, what would he obtain by it?'

He replied: 'O Satyakama, the syllable Om (AUM) is the highest and also the other Brahman; there he who knows it arrives by the same means at one of the two.

'If he meditates on one Matra (the A), then, being enlightened by that only, he arrives quickly at the earth. The Rik verses lead him to the world of men, and being endowed there with penance, abstinence, and faith, he enjoys greatness.

'If he meditates with two Matras (A+U) he arrives at the Manas, and is led up by the Yajus verses to the sky, to the Soma world. Having enjoyed greatness in the Soma world, he returns again.

'Again, he who meditates with this syllable AUM of three Matras, on the Highest Person, he comes to light and to the sun. And as a snake is freed from its skin, so is he freed from evil. He is led up by the Saman verses to the Brahma-world; and from him, full of life, Hiranyagarbha, the lord of the Satya-loka, he learns to see the all-pervading, the Highest Person. And there are these two Shlokas:

'The three Matras (A+U+M), if employed separate, and only joined one to another, are mortal; but in acts, external, or intermediate, if well performed, the sage trembles not.

'Through the Rik verses he arrives at this world, through the Yajus verses at the sky, through the Saman verses at that which the poets teach,—he arrives at this by means of the Omkara; the wise arrives at that which is at rest, free from decay, from death, from fear,—the Highest.'

Sixth Question

Then Sukeshas Bharadvaja asked him, saying: 'Sir, Hiranyanabha, the prince of Kosala, came to me and asked this question: Do you know the person of sixteen parts, O Bharadvaja? I said to the prince: I do not know him; if I knew him how should I not tell you? Surely, he who speaks what is untrue withers away to the very root; therefore I will not say what is untrue. Then he mounted his chariot and went away silently. Now I ask you, where is that person?'

He replied: 'Friend, that person is here within the body, he in whom these sixteen parts arise.

'He reflected: What is it by whose departure I shall depart, and by whose staying I shall stay?

'He sent forth Prana; from Prana came Sraddha (faith), ether, air, light, water, earth, sense, mind, food; from food came vigour, penance, hymns, sacrifice, the worlds, and in the worlds the name also.

'As these flowing rivers that go towards the ocean, when they have reached the ocean, sink into it, their name and form are broken, and people speak of the ocean only, exactly thus these sixteen parts of the spectator that go towards the Person (Purusha); when they have reached the Person, sink into him, their name and form are broken, and people speak of the Person only, and he becomes without parts and immortal. On this there is this verse:

'That Person who is to be known, he in whom these parts rest, like spokes in the nave of a wheel, you know him, lest death should hurt you.'

Then Pippalada said to them: 'So far do I know this Highest Brahman, there is nothing higher than it.'

And they, praising him, said: 'You, indeed, are our father, you who carry us from our ignorance to the other shore.'

Adoration to the highest Rishis!

Adoration to the highest Rishis!

Tat sat. Harih Om!

FLOWERS: The Essential Gita

The Doctrine

Krishna

How hath this weakness taken thee?
Whence springs
The inglorious trouble, shameful to the brave,
Barring the path of virtue? Nay, Arjuna!
Forbid thyself feebleness! it mars
Thy warrior-name! cast off the coward-fit!
Wake! Be thyself! Arise, Scourge of thy Foes!

Arjuna

How can I, in the battle, shoot with shafts
On Bhishma, or on Drona—O thou Chief!—
Better to live on beggar's bread
With those we love alive,
Than taste their blood in rich feasts spread,
And guiltily survive!
Ah! were it worse—who knows?—to be
Victor or vanquished here,
When those confront us angrily
Whose death leaves living drear?
In pity lost, by doubtings tossed,
My thoughts—distracted—turn
To Thee, the Guide I reverence most,

That I may counsel learn:
I know not what would heal the grief
Burned into soul and sense,
If I were earth's unchallenged chief—
A god—and these gone thence!

Sanjaya
So spake Arjuna to the Lord of Hearts,
And sighing, "I will ot fight!" held silence then.
To whom, with tender smile, (O Bharata!)
While the prince wept despairing 'twixt those hosts,
Krishna made answer in divinest verse:

Krishna
Thou grievest where no grief should be! thou speak'st
Words lacking wisdom! for the wise in heart
Mourn not for those that live, nor those that die.
Nor I, nor thou, nor anyone of these,
Ever was not, nor ever will not be,
For ever and for ever afterwards.
All, that doth live, lives always! To man's frame
As there come infancy and youth and age,
So come there raisings-up and laying-down
Of other and of other life-abodes,
Which the wise know, and fear not. This that irks—
Thy sense—life, thrilling to the elements—
Bringing thee heat and cold, sorrows and joys,
'Tis brief and mutable! Bear with it, Prince!
As the wise bear. The soul which is not moved,

The soul that with a strong and constant calm
Takes sorrow and takes joy indifferently,
Lives in the life undying! That which is
Can never cease to be; that which is not
Will not exist. To see this truth of both
Is theirs who part essence from accident,
Substance from shadow. Indestructible,
Learn thou! the Life is, spreading life through all;
It cannot anywhere, by any means,
Be anywise diminished, stayed, or changed.
But for these fleeing frames which it informs
With spirit deathless, endless, infinite,
They perish. Let them perish, Prince! and fight!
He who shall say, "Lo! I have slain a man!"
He who shall think, "Lo! I am slain!" those both
Know naught! Life cannot slay. Life is not slain!
Never the spirit was born; the spirit shall cease to
be never;
Never was time it was not; End and Beginning are
dreams!
Birthless and deathless and changeless remaineth
the spirit for ever;
Death hath not touched it at all, dead though the
house of it seems!
Who knoweth it exhaustless, self-sustained,
Immortal, indestructible—shall such
Say, "I have killed a man, or caused to kill?"

Nay, but as when one layeth
His worn-out robes away,
And, taking new ones, sayeth,
"These will I wear to-day!"
So putteth by the spirit
Lightly its garb of flesh,
And passeth to inherit
A residence afresh.

I say to thee weapons reach not the Life;
Flame burns it not, waters cannot O'erwhelm,
Nor dry winds wither it. Impenetrable,
Unentered, unassailed, unharmed, untouched,
Immortal, all-arriving, stable, sure,
Invisible, ineffable, by word
And thought uncompassed, ever all itself,
Thus is the Soul declared! How wilt thou, then,—
Knowing it so,—grieve when thou shouldst not grieve?
How, if thou hearest that the man new-dead
Is, like the man new-born, still living man—
One same, existent Spirit—wilt thou weep?
The end of birth is death; the end of death
Is birth: this is ordained! and mournest thou,
Chief of the stalwart arm! for what befalls
Which could not otherwise befall? The birth
Of living things comes unperceived; the death
Comes unperceived; between them, beings perceive:
What is there sorrowful herein, dear Prince?
Wonderful, wistful, to contemplate!

Difficult, doubtful, to speak upon!
Strange and great for tongue to relate,
Mystical hearing for everyone!
Nor knoweth man this, what a marvel it is,
When seeing, and saying, and hearing are done!

This life within all living things, my Prince!
Hides beyond harm; scorn thou to suffer, then,
For that which cannot suffer. Do thy part!
Be mindful of thy name, and tremble not!
Nought better can betide a martial soul
Than lawful war; happy the warrior
To whom comes joy of battle—comes, as now,
Glorious and fair, unsought; opening for him
A gateway unto Heav'n. But, if thou shunn'st
This honourable field—a Kshattriya—
If, knowing thy duty and thy task, thou bidd'st
Duty and task go by—that shall be sin!
And those to come shall speak thee infamy
From age to age; but infamy is worse
For men of noble blood to bear than death!
The chiefs upon their battle-chariots
Will deem't was fear that drove thee from the fray.
Of those who held thee mighty-souled the scorn
Thou must abide, while all thine enemies
Will scatter bitter speech on thee, to mock
The valour which thou hadst; what fate could fall
More grievously than this? Either—being killed—
Thou wilt win Swarga's safety, or—alive

And victor—thou wilt reign an earthly king.
Therefore, arise, thou Son of Kunti! brace
Thine arm for conflict, nerve thy heart to meet—
As things alike to thee—pleasure or pain,
Profit or ruin, victory or defeat:
So minded, gird thee to the fight, for so
Thou shalt not sin!

Thus far I speak to thee
As from the "Sankhya" — unspiritually—
Hear now the deeper teaching of the Yoga,
Which holding, understanding, thou shalt burst
Thy Karmabandh, the bondage of wrought deeds.
Here shall no end be hindered, no hope marred,
No loss be feared: faith—yea, a little faith—
Shall save thee from the anguish of thy dread.
Here, Glory of the Kurus! shines one rule—
One steadfast rule—while shifting souls have laws
Many and hard. Specious, but wrongful deem
The speech of those ill-taught ones who extol
The letter of their Vedas, saying "This
Is all we have, or need; "being weak at heart
With wants, seekers of Heaven: which comes—they say—
As "fruit of good deeds done;" promising men
Much profit in new births for works of faith;
In various rites abounding; following whereon
Large merit shall accrue towards wealth and power;
Albeit, who wealth and power do most desire
Least fixity of soul have such, least hold

On heavenly meditation. Much these teach,
From Vedas, concerning the "three qualities;"
But thou, be free of the "three qualities,"
Free of the "pairs of opposites," and free from that sad
righteousness which calculates;
Self-ruled, Arjuna! simple, satisfied!
Look! like as when a tank pours water forth
To suit all needs, so do these Brahmins draw
Text for all wants from tank of Holy Writ.
But thou, want not! ask not! Find full reward
Of doing right in right! **Let right deeds be**
Thy motive, not the fruit which comes from them.
And live in action! Labour! Make thine acts
Thy piety, casting all self aside,
Contemning gain and merit; equable
In good or evil: equability
Is Yoga, is piety!

Yet, the right act
Is less, far less, than the right thinking mind.
Seek refuge in thy soul; have there thy heaven!
Scorn them that follow virtue for her gifts!
The mind of pure devotion—even here—
Casts equally aside good deeds and bad,
Passing above them. Unto pure devotion
Devote thyself; with perfect meditation
Comes perfect act, and the right-hearted rise—
More certainly because they seek no gain—
Forth from the bonds of body, step by step,

To highest seats of bliss. When thy firm soul
Hath shaken off those tangled oracles
Which ignorantly guide, then shall it soar
To high neglect of what's denied or said,
This way or that way, in doctrinal writ.
Troubled no longer by the priestly lore,
Safe shall it live, and sure; steadfastly bent
On meditation. This is Yoga—and Peace!

Arjuna

What is his mark who hath that steadfast heart,
Confirmed in holy meditation? How
Know we his speech, Kesava? Sits he, moves he
Like other men?

Krishna

When one, O Pritha's Son!—
Abandoning desires which shake the mind—
Finds in his soul full comfort for his soul,
He hath attained the Yoga—that man is such!
In sorrows not dejected, and in joys
Not overjoyed; dwelling outside the stress
Of passion, fear, and anger; fixed in calms
Of lofty contemplation;—such an one
Is Muni, is the Sage, the true Recluse!
He who to none and nowhere overbound
By ties of flesh, takes evil things and good
Neither desponding nor exulting, such
Bears wisdom's plainest mark! He who shall draw

As the wise tortoise draws its four feet safe
Under its shield, his five frail senses back
Under the spirit's buckler from the world
Which else assails them, such an one, my Prince!
Hath wisdom's mark! Things that solicit sense
Hold off from the self-governed; nay, it comes,
The appetites of him who lives beyond
Depart,—aroused no more. Yet may it chance,
O Son of Kunti! that a governed mind
Shall some time feel the sense-storms sweep, and wrest
Strong self-control by the roots. Let him regain
His kingdom! let him conquer this, and sit
On Me intent. **That man alone is wise**
Who keeps the mastery of himself! If one
Ponders on objects of the sense, there springs
Attraction; from attraction grows desire,
Desire flames to fierce passion, passion breeds
Recklessness; then the memory—all betrayed—
Lets noble purpose go, and saps the mind,
Till purpose, mind, and man are all undone.
But, if one deals with objects of the sense
Not loving and not hating, making them
Serve his free soul!, which rests serenely lord,
Lo! such a man comes to tranquillity;
And out of that tranquillity shall rise
The end and healing of his earthly pains,
Since the will governed sets the soul at peace.
The soul of the ungoverned is not his,

Nor hath he knowledge of himself; which lacked,
How grows serenity? and, wanting that,
Whence shall he hope for happiness?

The mind
That gives itself to follow shows of sense
Seeth its helm of wisdom rent away,
And, like a ship in waves of whirlwind, drives
To wreck and death. Oniy with him, great Prince!
Whose senses are not swayed by things of sense—
Only with him who holds his mastery,
Shows wisdom perfect. What is midnight-gloom
To unenlightened souls shines wakeful day
To his clear gaze: what seems as wakeful day
Is known for night, thick night of ignorance,
To his true-seeing eyes. Such is the Saint!
And like the ocean, day by day receiving
Floods from all lands, which never overflows;
Its boundary-line not leaping, and not leaving,
Fed by the rivers, but unswelled by those;—
So is the perfect one! to his soul's ocean
The world of sense pours streams of witchery,
They leave him as they find, without commotion,
Taking their tribute, but remaining sea.

Yea! whoso, shaking off the yoke of flesh
Lives lord, not servant, of his lusts; set free
From pride, from passion, from the sin of "self",
Toucheth tranquillity! O Pritha's Son!

That is the state of Brahma! There rests no dread
When that last step is reached! Live where he will,
Die when he may, such passeth from all 'plaining,
To blest Nirvana, with the Gods, attaining.

(Ch.2)

The Royal Path

Krishna

Now will I open unto thee — whose heart
Rejects not — that last lore, deepest—concealed,
That farthest secret of My Heavens and Earths,
Which but to know shall set thee free from ills, —
A royal lore! a Kingly mystery!
Yea! for the soul such light as purgeth it
From every sin; a light of holiness
With inmost splendour shining; plain to see;
Easy to walk by, inexhaustible!

They that receive not this, failing in faith
To grasp the greater wisdom, reach not Me,
Destroyer of thy foes! They sink anew
Into the realm of Flesh, where all things change!

By Me the whole vast Universe of things
Is spread abroad; — by Me, the Unmanifest!
In Me are all existences contained;
Not I in them!

Yet they are not contained,
Those visible things! Receive and strive to embrace
The mystery majestical! My Being —
Creating all, sustaining all— still dwells
Outside of all!

See! as the shoreless airs
Move in the measureless space, but are not space,
(And space were space without the moving airs);
So all things are in Me, but are not I.

At closing of each Kalpa, Indian Prince!
All things which be back to My Being come:
At the beginning of each Kalpa, all
Issue new-born from Me.

By Energy
And help of Prakriti, my outer Self,
Again, and yet again, I make go forth
The realms of visible things — without their will—
All of them — by the power of Prakriti.
Yet these great makings, Prince! involve Me not,
Enchain Me not! I sit apart from them,
Other, and Higher, and Free; nowise attached!
Thus doth the stuff of worlds, moulded by Me,
Bring forth all that which is moving or still,
Living or lifeless! Thus the worlds go on!

The minds untaught mistake Me, veiled in form; —
Naught see they of My secret Presence, nought
Of My hid Nature, ruling all which lives.
Vain hopes pursuing, vain deeds doing; fed
On vainest knowledge, senselessly they seek
An evil way, the way of brutes and fiends.
But My Mahatmas, those of noble soul

Who tread the path celestial, worship Me
With hearts unwandering, — knowing Me the Source,
Th' Eternal Source, of Life. Unendingly
They glorify Me; seek Me; keep their vows
Of reverence and love, with changeless faith
Adoring Me. Yea, and those too adore,
Who, offering sacrifice of wakened hearts,
Have sense of one pervading Spirit's stress,
One Force in every place, though manifold!
I am the Sacrifice! I am the Prayer!
I am the Funeral-Cake set for the dead!
I am the healing herb! I am the ghee,
The Mantra, and the flame, and that which burns!
I am — of all this boundless Universe—
The Father, Mother, Ancestor, and Guard!
The end of Learning! That which purifies
In lustral water! I am OM! I am
Rig-Veda, Sama-Veda, Yajur-Veda;
The Way, the Fosterer, the Lord, the Judge,
The Witness; the Abode, the Refuge-House,
The Friend, the Fountain and the Sea of Life
Which sends, and swallows up; Treasure of Worlds
And Treasure-Chamber! Seed and Seed-Sower,
Whence endless harvests spring! Sun's heat is mine;
Heaven's rain is mine to grant or to withhold;
Death am I, and Immortal Life I am,
Arjuna! SAT and ASAT, Visible Life,
And Life Invisible!

Yea! those who learn
The threefold Vedas, who drink the Soma-wine,
Purge sins, pay sacrifice — from Me they earn
Passage to SWARGA; where the meats divine
Of great gods feed them in high Indra's heaven.
Yet they, when that prodigious joy is o'er,
Paradise spent, and wage for merits given,
Come to the world of death and change once more.
They had their recompense! they stored their treasure,
Following the threefold Scripture and its writ;
Who seeketh such gaineth the fleeting pleasure
Of joy which comes and goes! I grant them it!

But to those blessed ones who worship Me,
Turning not otherwhere, with minds set fast,
I bring assurance of full bliss beyond.

Nay, and of hearts which follow other gods
In simple faith, their prayers arise to me,
O Kunti's Son! though they pray wrongfully;
For I am the Receiver and the Lord
Of every sacrifice, which these know not
Rightfully; so they fall to earth again!
Who follow gods go to their gods; who vow
Their souls to Pitris go to Pitris; minds
To evil Bhuts given o'er sink to the Bhuts;
And whoso shall offer Me in faith and love
A leaf, a flower, a fruit, water poured forth,

That offering I accept, lovingly made
With pious will. Whate'er thou doest, Prince!
Eating or sacrificing, giving gifts,
Praying or fasting, let it all be done
For Me, as Mine. So shalt thou free thyself
From Karmabandh, the chain which holdeth men
To good and evil issue, so shalt come
Safe unto Me — when thou art quit of flesh —
By faith and abdication joined to Me!

I am alike for all! I know not hate,
I know not favour! What is made is Mine!
But them that worship Me with love, I love;
They are in Me, and I in them!

Nay, Prince!
If one evil life turn in his thought
Straightly to Me, count him amidst the good;
He hath the high way chosen; he shall grow
Righteous ere long; he shall attain that peace
Which changes not. Thou Prince of India!
Be certain none can perish, trusting Me!
O Pritha's Son! whoso will turn to Me,
Though they be born from the very womb of Sin,
Woman or man; sprung of the Vaisya caste
Or lowly disregarded Sudra, — all
Plant foot upon the highest path; how then
The holy Brahmins and My Royal Saints?
Ah! ye who into this ill world are come —

Fleeting and false — set your faith fast on Me!
Fix heart and thought on Me! Adore Me! Bring
Offerings to Me! Make Me prostrations! Make
Me your supremest joy! and, undivided,
Unto My rest your spirits shall be guided.

(Ch.9)

The Path of Perfection

Krishna

Hear farther yet, thou Long-Armed Lord! these latest words I say —

Uttered to bring thee bliss and peace, who lovest Me always—

Not the great company of gods nor kingly Rishis know

My Nature, Who have made the gods and Rishis long ago;

He only knoweth — only he is free of sin, and wise,

Who seeth Me, Lord of the Worlds, with faith-enlightened eyes,

Unborn, undying, unbegun. Whatever natures be

To mortal men distributed, those natures spring from Me!

Intellect, skill, enlightenment, endurance, self-control,

Truthfulness, equability, and grief or joy of soul,

And birth and death, and fearfulness, and fearlessness, and shame,

And honour, and sweet harmlessness, and peace which is the same

Whate'er befalls, and mirth, and tears, and piety, and thrift,

And wish to give, and will to help, — all cometh of My gift!

The Seven Chief Saints, the Elders Four, the Lordly Manus set —

Sharing My work — to rule the worlds, these too did I beget;

And Rishis, Pitris, Manus, all, by one thought of My mind;

Thence did arise, to fill this world, the races of mankind;

Wherefrom who comprehends My Reign of mystic Majesty—That truth of truths—is thenceforth linked in fault- less faith to Me:

Yea! knowing Me the source of all, by Me all creatures wrought,

The wise in spirit cleave to Me, into My Being brought;

Hearts fixed on Me; breaths breathed to Me; praising Me, each to each,

So have they happiness and peace, with pious thought and speech;

And unto these — thus serving well, thus loving ceaselessly —

I give a mind of perfect mood, whereby they draw to Me;

And, all for love of them, within their darkened souls I dwell,

And, with bright rays of wisdom's lamp, their

ignorance dispel.

Arjuna

Yes! Thou art Parabrahma! The High Abode!

The Great Purification! Thou art God

Eternal, All-creating, Holy, First,

Without beginning! Lord of Lords and Gods!

Declared by all the Saints — by Narada,

Vyasa, Asita, and Devalas;

And here Thyself declaring unto me!
What Thou hast said now know I to be truth,
O Kesava! that neither gods nor men
Nor demons comprehend Thy mystery
Made manifest, Divinest! Thou Thyself,
Thyself alone dost know, Maker Supreme!
Master of all the living! Lord of Gods!
King of the Universe! To Thee alone
Belongs to tell the heavenly excellence
Of those perfections wherewith Thou dost fill
These worlds of Thine; Pervading, Immanent!
How shall I learn, Supremest Mystery!
To know Thee, though I muse continually?
Under what form of thine unnumbered forms
Mayst Thou be grasped? Ah! yet again recount,
Clear and complete, Thy great appearances,
The secrets of Thy Majesty and Might,
Thou high Delight of Men! Never enough
Can mine ears drink the Amrit of such words!

Krishna

Hanta! So be it! Kuru Prince! I will to thee unfold
Some portions of My Majesty, whose powers are manifold!
I am the Spirit seated deep in every creature's heart;
From Me they come; by Me they live; at My word they depart!
Vishnu of the Adityas I am, those Lords of Light;
Maritchi of the Maruts, the Kings of Storm and Blight;

By day I gleam, the golden Sun of burning cloudless Noon,
By Night, amid the asterisms I glide, the dappled Moon'
Of Vedas I am Sama-Veda, of gods in Indra's Heaven
Vasava; Of the faculties to living beings given
The mind which apprehends and thinks; of Rudras Sankara,
Of Yakshas and of Rakshasas, Vittesh; and Pavaka
Of Vasus, and of mountain-peaks Meru; Brihaspati
Know Me 'mid planetary Powers; 'mid Warriors heavenly
Skanda; of all the water-floods the Sea which drinketh each,
And Bhrigu of the holy Saints, and OM of sacred speech,
Of prayers the prayer ye whisper; of hills Himala's snow,
And Aswattha, the fig-tree, of all the trees that grow;
Of the Devarshis, Narada; and Chitrarath of them
That sing in Heaven, and Kapila of Munis, and the gem.
Of flying steeds, Uchchaisravas, from Amrit-wave which burst;
Of elephants Airavata; of males the Best and First;
Of weapons Heav'n's hot thunderbolt; of cows white Kamadhuk,
From whose great milky udder-teats all hearts' desires are strook;
Vasuki of the serpent-tribes, round Mandara entwined;
And thousand-fanged Ananta, on whose broad coils reclined
Leans Vishnu; and of water-things Varuna; Aryama
Of Pitris, and, of those that judge, Yama the Judge I am;
Of Daityas dread Prahlada; of what metes days and years,

Time's self I am; of woodland-beasts — buffaloes, deers, and bears —

The lordly-painted tiger; of birds the vast Garud,

The whirlwind 'mid the winds; 'mid chiefs Rama with blood imbrued,

Makar 'mid fishes of the sea, and Ganges 'mid the streams;

Yes! First, and Last, and Centre of all which is or seems

I am, Arjuna! Wisdom Supreme of what is wise, Words on the uttering lips I am, and eyesight of the eyes,

And "A" of written characters, Dwandwa of knitted speech.

And Endless Life, and boundles Love, whose power sustaineth each;

And bitter Death which seizes all, and joyous sudden Birth,

Which brings to light all beings that are to be on earth;

And of the viewless virtues, Fame, Fortune, Song am I,

And Memory, and Patience; and Craft, and Constancy:

Of Vedic hymns the Vrihatsam, of metres Gayatri, Of months the Margasirsha, of all the seasons three

The flower-wreathed Spring; in dicer's-play the conquering Double-Eight;

The splendour of the splendid, and the greatness of the great.

Victory I am, and Action! and the goodness of the good,
And Vasudev of Vrishni's race, and of this Pandu brood

Thyself! — Yea, my Arjuna! thyself; for thou art Mine!

Of poets Usana, of saints Vyasa, sage divine;

The policy of conquerors, the potency of kings, The great unbroken silence in learning's secret things,

The lore of all the learned, the seed of all which springs.

Living or lifeless, still or stirred, whatever beings be,
None of them is in all the worlds, but it exists by Me

Nor tongue can tell Arjuna! nor end of telling come

Of these My boundless glories, whereof I teach thee some;

For wheresoe'er is wondrous work, and majesty, and might,

From Me hath all proceeded. Receive thou this aright!

Yet how shouldst thou receive, O Prince! the vastness of this world?

I, who am all, and made it all, abide its separate Lord!

(Ch.10)

The Glory of God

Arjuna

This, for my soul's peace, have I heard from Thee,
The unfolding of the Mystery Supreme
Named Adhyatman; comprehending which,
My darkness is dispelled; for now I know —
O Lotus-eyed!+ — whence is the birth of men,
And whence their death, and what the majesties
Of Thine immortal rule. Fain would I see,
As thou Thyself declar'st it, Sovereign Lord!
The likeness of that glory of Thy Form
Wholly revealed. O Thou Divinest One!
If this can be, if I may bear the sight,
Make Thyself visible, Lord of all prayers!
Show me Thy very self, the Eternal God!

Krishna

Gaze, then, thou Son of Pritha! I manifest for thee
Those hundred thousand thousand shapes that clothe
my Mystery:

I show thee all my semblances, infinite, rich, divine,
My changeful hues, my countless forms.
See in this face of mine.

Adityas, Vasus, Rudras, Aswins, and Maruts; see
Wonders unnumbered, India Prince!
Revealed to none save thee.

Behold! this is the Universe! - Look!
What is live and dead

I gather all in one - in Me! Gaze, as thy lips have said,

On GOD ETERNAL, VERY GOD! See Me!
See what thou prayest!

Thou can't not! - nor, with human eyes,
See you ever mayest!

Therefore I give thee sense divine.
Have other eyes, new light!

And, look! This is My glory, unveiled to mortal sight!

Sanjaya

Then, O King! the God, so saying,
Stood, to Pritha's Son displaying
All the splendour, wonder, dread
Of His vast Almighty—head.
Out of countless eyes beholding,
Out of countless months commanding,
Countless mystic forms enfolding
In one Form: supremely standing
Countless radiant glories wearing,
Countless heavenly weapons bearing,
Crowned with garlands of star-clusters,
Robed in garb of woven lustres,
Breathing from His perfect Presence
Breaths of every subtle essence
Of all heavenly odours; shedding
Blinding brilliance; overspreading —
Boundless, beautiful—all spaces
With His all-regarding faces;
So He showed! If there should rise

Suddenly within the skies
Sunburst of a thousand suns
Flooding earth with beams undeemed of,
Then might be that Holy One's
Majesty and radiance dreamed of!

So did Pandu's son behold
All this universe enfold
All its huge diversity
Into one vast shape, and be
Visible, and viewed, and blended
In one Body — subtle, splendid,
Nameless — th' All-comprehending
God of Gods, the Never-Ending Deity!

But, sore amazed,
Thrilled, o'erfilled, dazzled, and dazed,
Arjuna knelt; and bowed his head,
And clasped his palms; and cried, and said:

Arjuna

Yea! I have seen! I see!
Lord! all is wrapped in Thee!
The gods are in Thy glorious frame! the creatures
Of earth, and heaven, and hell
In Thy Divine form dwell,
And in Thy countenance shine all the features

Of Brahma, sitting lone
Upon His lotus-throne;

Of saints and sages, and the serpent races
Ananta, Vasuki;
Yea! mightiest Lord! I see
Thy thousand arms, and breasts, and faces,

And eyes, — on every side Perfect, diversified;
And nowhere end of Thee, nowhere beginning,
Nowhere a centre! Shifts—
Wherever Soul's gaze lifts—
Thy central Self, all-wielding, and all-winning!

Infinite King! I see
The anadem on Thee,
The club, the shell, the discus; see Thee burning
In beams insufferable,
Lighting earth, heaven, and hell
With brilliance blazing, glowing, flashing; turning
Darkness to dazzling day,
Look I whichever way;
Ah, Lord! I worship Thee, the Undivided,
The Uttermost of thought,
The Treasure-Palace wrought
To hold the wealth of the worlds; the Shield provided
To shelter Virtue's laws;
The Fount whence Life's stream draws
All Waters of all rivers of all being:
The One Unborn, Unending;
Unchanging and Unblending!
With might and majesty, past thought, past seeing!

Silver of moon and gold
Of sun are glories rolled
From Thy great eyes; Thy visage, beaming tender
Throughout the stars and skies,
Doth to warm life surprise
Thy Universe. The worlds are filled with wonder
Of Thy perfections! Space
Star-sprinkled, and void place
From pole to pole of the Blue, from bound to bound,
Hath Thee in every spot,
Thee, Thee! — Where Thou art not,
O Holy, Marvellous Form! is nowhere found!

O Mystic, Awful One!
At sight of Thee, made known,
The Three Worlds quake; the lower gods draw nigh Thee;
They fold their palms, and bow
Body, and breast, and brow,
And, whispering worship, laud and magnify Thee!

Rishis and Siddhas cry
"Hail! Highest Majesty!"
From sage and singer breaks the hymn of glory
In dulcet harmony,
Sounding the praise of Thee;
While countless companies take up the story,

Rudras, who ride the storms,
Th' Adityas' shining forms,

Vasus and Sadhyas, Viswas, Ushmapas;
Maruts, and those great Twins
The heavenly, fair, Aswins,
Gandharvas, Rakshasas, Siddhas, and Asuras,

These see Thee, and revere
In sudden-stricken fear;
Yea! the Worlds, — seeing Thee with form stupendous,
With faces manifold,
With eyes which all behold,
Unnumbered eyes, vast arms, members tremendous,

Flanks, lit with sun and star,
Feet planted near and far,
Tushes of terror, mouths wrathful and tender; —
The Three wide Worlds before Thee
Adore, as I adore Thee,
Quake, as I quake, to witness so much splendour!

I mark Thee strike the skies
With front, in wondrous wise
Huge, rainbow-painted, glittering, and thy mouth
Opened, and orbs which see
All things, whatever be
In all Thy worlds, east, west, and north and south.

O Eyes of God! O Head!
My strength of soul is fled,

Gone is heart's force, rebuked is mind's desire!
When I behold Thee so,
With awful brows a-glow,
With burning glance, and lips lighted by fire

Fierce as those flames which shall
Consume, at close of all,
Earth, Heaven! Ah me! I see no Earth and Heaven!
Thee, Lord of Lords! I see,
Thee only — only Thee!
Now let Thy mercy unto me be given.

Thou Refuge of the World!
Lo! to the cavern hurled
Of Thy wide-opened throat, and lips white-tushed,
I see our noblest one,
Great Dhritarashtra's sons,
Bhishma, Drona, and Karna, caught and crushed!

The Kings and Chiefs drawn in,
That gaping gorge within;
The best of both these armies torn and riven!
Between Thy jaws they lie
Mangled full bloodily,
Ground into dust and death! Like streams down-driven

With helpless haste, which go
In headlong furious flow
Straight to the gulfing deeps of th' unfilled ocean,

So to that flaming cave
Those heroes great and brave
Pour, in unending streams, with helpless motion!

Like moths which in the night
Flutter towards a light,
Drawn to their fiery doom, flying and dying,
So to their death still throng,
Blind, dazzled, borne along
Ceaselessly, all those multitudes, wild flying!

Thou, that hast fashioned men,
Devourest them again,
One with another, great and small, alike!
The creatures whom Thou mak'st,
With flaming jaws Thou tak'st,
Lapping them up! Lord God! Thy terrors strike

From end to end of earth,
Filling life full, from birth
To death, with deadly, burning, lurid dread!
Ah Vishnu! make me know
Why is Thy visage so?
Who art Thou, feasting thus upon Thy dead?

Who? awful Deity!
I bow myself to Thee,
Namostu Te, Devavara! PrasidP
O Mightiest Lord! rehearse

Why hast Thou face so fierce?
Whence doth this aspect horrible proceed?

Krishna

Thou seest Me as Time who kills, Time who brings all to doom,

The Slayer Time, Ancient of Days, come hither to consume;

Excepting thee, of all these hosts of hostile chiefs arrayed,

There stands not one shall leave alive the battlefield! Dismayed

No Longer be! Arise! obtain renown! destroy thy foes!

Fight for the kingdom waiting thee when thou hast vanquished those,

By Me they fall — not thee! the stroke of death is dealt them now,

Even as show thus gallantly; My instrument art thou!

Strike, strong-armed Prince, at Drona! at Bhishma strike! deal death

On Karna, Jayadratha; stay all their warlike breath!

'Tis I who bid them perish! Thou wilt but slay the slain;

Fight! they must fall, and thou must live, victor

Upon this plane.

(Ch.11)

Concepts of Hinduism

Advaita Vedanta —	The monistic tradition promoted by Sankara, that the sole reality is Brahman, the impersonal Absolute, Nirguna, without qualities. The world is Maya, illusion, and the Brahman and the Self are one.
Ahimsa —	Non-violence, non-injury, advocated by ascetic traditions, later on by Mahatma Gandhi in political behaviour.
Ananda —	Bliss-elated consciousness, regarded also as the basic condition of creation.
Ananta —	Endless, the state of Time.
Artha —	The second goal of the four Purusharthas, the goals of Humanity, the effort to make one's living.
Atman —	Self, soul of a person, which is eternal and unchanging.
Avatara —	God's imcarnation in the world in human or any other form.
Bhakti —	Devotion to God.
Brahmacharya —	Celibacy, but essentially one's conduct according to Brahman, the first of the four stages of human life.
Brahman —	The power underlying all existence, the ultimate Reality, which can be Nirguna, without qualities, or

Saguna, with qualities, depending on one's world view, monistic or theistic.

Chitta — The conscious mind.

Darshana — Philosophy, There are six orthodox darshanas in Hinduism.

Dharma — Religion, social and religious duties.

Dhyana — Meditation, The 7th stage in the eight stages of Raja Yoga.

Dvaita Vedanta — Dualistic concept of Vedanta, promoled by Madhva, that the Brahman and Atman are two identities, the former being Vishnu.

Guna — Attribute, quality. The three gunas of Prakriti (Nature) are: Sattva (Purity), Rajas (Energy) and Tamas (Inertia).

Ishvara — God, Lord, the supreme

Jati — Caste or birth-group, sharing common lineage and customs.

Jiva — Individual soul or self, life.

Jivanmukti — The state of being liberated while still living.

Kaivalya — The state of Samadhi, separation of the Self from the body of a person.

Kama — Eros, desire, the third of the four Purusharthas, goals of humanity.

Karma — Action, deed. The theory that good Karma will result in good and bad Karma will result in bad life conditions in future births. All Hindu, Buddhistic and Jain traditions accept it.

Kundalini —	Divine force lying at the bottom of the spine in coiled form. It can be awakened and channeled through the chakras to rise to the forehead to attain liberation from rebirth.
Lila —	Play. The world is regarded as God's play for the sake of enjoyment.
Linga —	The symbolic representation of God Shiva in phallic form.
Mandala —	Diagram of squares, circles and triangles made to meditate.
Mantra —	A simgle or more words pronounced in special sounds to pray or meditate.
Maya —	Illusion, The nature of the phenomenal world, as Sankara has used it. We see the world as separate entities because of the power of Maya while all is Brahman.
Moksha —	Salvation or liberation from the bonds of life and rebirth.
Muni —	A sage who performs ascetic practices.
Om —	A blending of three sounds — A, U, M, — which represents all sound and is the key to union with the Absolute, Brahman. All the mantras start with it.
Panchmakara —	The five Ms as prononnced in Sanskrit, Maans (meat), Matsya (fish), Mudra (parched grain), Mada (alcohol) and Maithuna (sexual intercourse). Practised in left-hand tantric system.
Prakriti —	Nature, matter. As distinct from Purusha (Self) according to Samkhya philosophy.

Prana — Breath. One of the five forms of Life-energies. Prana (ascending breath), Apana (descending breath), Vyana (diffused breath), Udana (upward breath) and Samana (breath of the abdomen). These control upper and lower parts of the body, belching, speech, digestion, etc.

Pranayama — The fourth aspect of the eightfold Raja Yoga system, to control and manipulate the breathing system to cleanse the body and hold the mind to attain enlightenment.

Puja — The act of worshipping gods. A central religious ritual in which the deity is honoured, bathed and fed, and praised to receive benefits.

Punarjanma — Rebirth in accord to the Karma performed in life. A central belief of Hinduism, Jainism and Buddhism, which the West finds quite attractive these days.

Punya — Merit, result of good actions leading to better rebirth.

Purusha — Person, Self or Soul equivalent to Atman or Brahman or God.

Purushartha — The four aims of human life: Dharma, Artha, Kama and Moksha.

Rishi — Vedic seer. The hymns of the Vedas are attributed to the inspired seers who are said to have 'seen' the eternal truths and passed them on to humanity.

Rita — Cosmic order which operates automatically.

Sadhu —	Holy man or sage.
Samadhi —	The eighth and final stage in Raja Yoga where union with Brahman is attained.
Sannyasa —	The stage of renouncing everything and work for one's liberation from the bonds of life. The fourth and last stage of human life.
Samsara —	The cycle of life and death.
Samskara —	The twelve rites of human life as described in the Dharma Shastras.
Shanti —	Peace. A word of benediction.
Siddha —	A liberated person, or a person who has acquired extraordinary powers through yogic or tantric practices.
Shraddha —	Offerings to deceased ancestors in the form of food and water, performed according to religious rites.
Tapa —	Severe ascetic practices.
Upanayana —	Ceremony of receiving the sacred thread, one of the twelve samskaras.
Vanaprastha —	The third of the four stages of life, dwelling in the forest.
Varna —	Social group, there are four varnas in Hindu society: Brahmin, Kshatriya, Vaishya and Shudra.
Varnashrama —	The Hindu system consisting of four varnas—Brahmin, Kshatriya, Vaishya and Shudra—and four Ashramas—Brahmacharya, Grihastha, Vanaprastha and Sannyasa.

Vishisthadvaita Vedanta— Qualified Non-dualistic Vedanta, as propounded by Ramanuja, that Brahman is also Vishnu, the impersonal is also personal God, human beings his attributes separated from him due to ignorance, who with devotion or his grace can again unite with him.

Yajna — Vedic Sacrifices. An elaborate system by means of which human beings could have access to gods. The Aryans believed that fire would carry their offerings to them, invite them and please them.

Yoga — Physical and mental practices developed in ancient times to attain union with Brahman. The eightfold Raja Yoga was the most prominent, and is described in the Yoga Sutra of Patanjali. Its more severe variety is known as Hatha Yoga, still practised among various sects. There are many other forms and new ones are being created by intelligent experimenters. Sri Aurobindo developed Integral Yoga to acquire the further stage in human evolution on the earth. In modern times the word Yoga has become the central idea/symbol of Hinduism in the world.

Timeline

B C	
2500—1700	Indus Valley Civilisation
1500—1200	Aryans in India
1200—1000	Aryans spread to Yamuna and Ganga valleys, Rigveda compiled
6th Century	Gautama Buddha (563-483) lived, the age of Upanishads begins
5th Century	The age of sutras begins
4th Century	Panini the grammarian, Alexander's invasion and retreat (327-325) Chandragupta Maurya ruled north India (323-297), writing of Artha Shastra by Kautilya
3rd Century	King Asoka (271-231) ruled the country
2nd Century	Shunga Dynasty
1st Century	King Vikramaditya, start of Vikrama Era (58-57)
A D	
1st Century	Manav Dharma Shastra composed,
2nd Century	Lakulisa founds Pashupata sect, Ramayana completed
3rd Century	Pallava dynasty (3rd to 9th cent.) in Tamil Nadu. Hindu immigration to S.East Asia and their cultural influence in those lands
4th Century	Mahabharata completed, Puranas begin. Gupta dynasty (320-500) in the north, Chalukya dynasty in the south (4th through 6th centuries).

5th Century	Kalidasa
6th Century	Nayanar poets in the South
7th Century	Alvar poets, Mamallapuram temples
8th Century	Caves of Ellora carved, Muslims occupy Sind (Pakistan)
9th Century	Sankara, Advaita Vedanta philosopher. Nammalvar, Manikkavachakar, both Tamil saints
10th Century	Constuction of Chidambaram temple, Khajuraho temples
11th Century	Somnath temple destructed. Al-Biruni's visit
12th Century	Angkor Vat built in Cambodia, Basava starts Lingayata sect in Kannada, Jagannath temple completed in Puri, Ramanuja, Nimbarka, Jaidev.
13th Century	Surya temple in Konarak built, Madhvacharya
14th Century	Vijaynagara founded, Chandidas, Ramananda
15th Century	Kabir, Raidas
16th Century	Chaitanya, Mirabai, Vallabhacharya, Mughal Dynasty established, Tulsi Das
17th Century	Shivaji and Govind Singh, Aurangzeb's destructive policies, East India Company starts trading
18th Century	Asiatic Society of Bengal founded (1784) in Calcutta by Sir William Jones
19th Century	Brahmo Samaj founded (1828) by Ram Mohan Roy, war of independence in 1857, British government starts to govern the country in 1858, Arya Samaj

founded (1875) by Dayanand Saraswati, Theosophical Socity founded (1875) by Madame Blavatsky and Col. Olcott, Ramakrishna Paramahansa (1836-86), Vive-kananda (1863-1902) speaks at the Parliament of Religions in Chicago (1893) and founds Vedanta Society (1895)

20th Century	Mahatma Gandhi (1869-1948), Rabindranath Tagore (1860-1941) wins Nobel Prize (1913), Sri Aurobindo (1872-1950), Jawaharlal Nehru (1889-1964), B.R. Ambedkar (1893-1956), S. Radhakrishnan (1888-1975), India wins freedom (1947), Anandamayi Ma (1896-1987), Swami Muktananda (1908-82), Ananda Marg founded (1955), ISKCON founded in New York (1966) by Bhaktivedanta Swami Prabhupada, Maharishi Mahesh Yogi (1911-2008) founds Transcendenal Meditation system, Satya Sai Baba (1926—).

■■■